Abo

Standing at 6ft 1in and almost as wide, with a 23-inch neck, John 'The Neck' Houchin, as he was aptly known, rose from boarding school graduate to a club bouncing brawler in the 70s and 80s, minding the roughest and toughest of London's torrid and sometimes ungovernable dancehalls. Now 57 and living in Yorkshire, this is his first book.

THE
WITH LEE WORTLEY AND ANTHONY THOMAS
GUV'NOR AND ME

JOHN 'The Neck' HOUCHIN

EBURY
PRESS

1

Ebury Press, an imprint of Ebury Publishing
20 Vauxhall Bridge Road
London SW1V 2SA

Ebury Press is part of the Penguin Random House group of companies
whose addresses can be found at global.penguinrandomhouse.com

Penguin
Random House
UK

First published by Ebury Press in 2021

www.penguin.co.uk

A CIP catalogue record for this book is available from the British Library

ISBN 9781529107036

Typeset in 10.12/16.75 pt ITC Galliard Std
by Integra Software Services Pvt. Ltd, Pondicherry

Printed and bound in Great Britain by Clays Ltd, Elcograf S.p.A.

The authorised representative in the EEA is Penguin Random House
Ireland, Morrison Chambers, 32 Nassau Street, Dublin D02 YH68.

Contents

FOREWORD
BY AL CROSSLEY,
BRITAIN'S STRONGEST
MAN, 1984

I was first introduced to my dear friend, John, or Johnny boy as I like to call him, around 1986. I remember the year well because it was at the same time that I had just beaten Dave 'Man Mountain York' in under a minute during an unlicenced fight at Woodford Town Football Club. Shortly after, I was offered a bit of work in a place called Stocks. On my first night at the club, there was this young, up-and-coming bodybuilder who they called 'The Neck', a nickname I am sure you would all find befitting if indeed you had ever seen a photograph of him. Unlike these other big, loud doormen out to make a reputation for themselves, the kind of troublemakers you read about daily, well, our Johnny boy was different, unassuming without a hint of bravado, softly spoken and extremely polite. Because of this, and many other attributes found in John's personality, he and I hit it off right from the start. If we were ever working at different venues, we would make a point of popping round to see one another for a chat. This kindred spirit, born with a similar attitude and loyalty to mine, was why our friendship grew stronger overnight.

John and I ended up working some real rough houses together. The assurance that he and I would always have one another's back was forged through combats, those of which we fought shoulder to shoulder. My reputation in London has always been remarked upon, not just because I succeeded the great Geoff Capes, and won Britain's Strongest Man in 1984, but for my work as a minder and enforcer working alongside The Guv'nor, Lenny McLean. Not to mention a great many other hard men that I worked with, from Coleraine to the bright lights of London's West End. Therefore, when Johnny boy was coming up through the ranks as a well-respected minder and bodybuilding fighter himself, I immediately took him on board, and his apprenticeship began.

Johnny boy was a sharp lad and he knew when, and when not, to interject in any given situation. He would soak up every last nuance of knowledge that I threw at him and would always ask if he had done a specific something correctly. I remember one day, years ago, Johnny and I were sitting alone recalling many old memories over a nice cup of tea when one of us happened to bring up the idea of how good it would be to write a book; a book filled with the funny tales and stories from the many hours we had spent together, thoughts for years forgotten, from the far recesses of my mind. One that stands out quite prominently is the time when Johnny and I had been in a tear up with a bunch of loudmouth travelling men and, momentarily, after smashing them all up, Johnny boy snapped a pair of legs off one of the bar stools that he'd been using on the men and started spinning one in each of his hands like some gunslinger from a 1950s cowboy movie.

I also remember their little Shih Tzu dog, with its lion's heart. Now, without sounding paranoid, I'm sure that their little Tasmanian devil of a dog had it in for me because one day it almost kept me from leaving their family home. It's laughable, I know, for a well-known hard man to be held hostage by a ball of fluff with an attitude and, if I close my eyes, I can still see Johnny boy's beautiful better half, Dana, laughing hysterically as she watched on from the doorway. I spent a lot of time with John and his little family, and not just, as Johnny boy would claim, because Dana would cook and serve up a feast on my every visit. No, joking apart, while doing the doors and collecting debts together for a significant number of years, my pal John and I were inseparable. It's not often in this life you find a friend with the same morals and scruples as yourself.

Many people would come into the club and ask if John and I were brothers. This was, of course, a fantastic compliment for me, seeing as I was twelve years his senior. For me, this was invaluable ammunition to wind John up with, as I informed whoever was asking the question that John was my older brother, or maybe even my dad if I could get away with it.

John was a well-respected hard man, and he left a mark at whatever place he worked; he had strength and power with a fantastic amount of speed, especially for a man of his size.

Johnny boy was also a charismatic, streetwise, and larger-than-life character. Although in life everyone moves on, and some people lose touch with one another, John and I have remained friends to this day. We regularly speak on the phone, and we are both aware that if something went a little boss-eyed for either one of us, then the other would be by his side at the drop of a hat. I felt privileged to have been asked to write the foreword for his fascinating book. Nevertheless, there is only one thing I do best with my hands, and I think you all know what that is. So, with that in mind, I have left the polishing up and finer details of this foreword in the safe hands of the writers, Lee and Anthony.

Now, sit back, and I'll let the man himself tell you the rest. A man who began life as a skinny little bullied kid from Hayes, and quickly grew into one of the most formidable enforcers London has ever produced. To me, however, he is simply my dear friend, Johnny boy, yet to you he will always remain, 'John the Neck'.

1
A BOARDING PASS TO THE WEST END

Let us go back to the beginning, back to the year that I was brought into this world, which was 27 June 1963 in Hayes, west London. It was the year in which Bruce Reynolds masterminded the £2.6 million Great Train Robbery, and also the year our very own John, Paul, George and Ringo bust their way out of Penny Lane and found their voice, nationally. My parents were my labourer and driver dad, Maurice Houchin, and my stay-at-home mum, Valerie Bond. Bond was, of course, Mum's maiden name and indeed a widely iconic name in the world of British intelligence and espionage, which brings with it a fact of some interest; my shaken but not stirred grandfather was, in fact, named James Bond – a truth that served me well with my pals in the playground.

I had a strict and sometimes brutal adolescent life. I was born into a typical post-war, working-class family consisting of the five of us: me, Mum, Dad, my younger brother Michael and older sister Winifred, or Win, as we called her.

I was a little different to my brother and sister – this was all apparent from an early age with the onset of my childhood asthma and an inner ear problem, causing me to behave a little wild at times. Maybe this explains the reason why I, out of the three of us, was packed off to boarding school at the innocent age of four. This decision was established by my parents, albeit with the leaden hand of my father's totalitarian approach influencing my mother. In the sixties, this was the way of all families' decision making.

I guess a part of my feelings at that time was, why me? Out of the three of us, why would I be singled out to the life of school with board? Am I the black sheep of the family or something? However, any thought in that direction immediately came and went once something of more interest came into my psyche. Maybe it was the total opposite of this – perhaps I was singled out because they simply wanted more for me. At the time, it did not occur to me to question such a decision – here, look, this was between the ages of four and twelve, I don't suppose I really cared. I was probably too busy pulling girls' ponytails and running around fighting to dwell on such issues.

But, yes, I did indeed feel that I was treated a little differently to my brother and sister, which is something that I have never discussed with either of them. For all intents and purposes, my father always seemed a little resentful towards me. If anyone ever praised me, for example, my dad would always try and find a point of negativity to it. I suppose I felt that my sister could do no wrong, but was it that, or was it because I was just a right handful and they never knew how to deal with me? In my mum's eyes I was simply her slightly broken little boy, and we all know that in the eyes of a mother their sweet son can do no wrong. But for whatever reason they chose to adopt I was, shall we say, singled out. And for better or worse it was, at this moment in time, my destiny.

The morning of my first day of school was like any other – it was up and out of bed, a quick, regimented itinerary of breakfast, bath, teeth brushed, and hair combed, and I'm all set for my new life in a new town, and whatever else was to come.

So, there I was, suitcase in hand, with the subtlest of goodbyes, as I'm packed off to a world of *Flashman* and a *Tom Brown's Schooldays*-esque life for me to grow up in. I was never really fazed by this new world because, let's face it, at the tender age of four, I had no idea what was coming. For all I knew, I could have been going off to a world of Charlie and his factory of chocolate, Tolkien's Middle-earth, or maybe even the witches and wardrobes of Narnia.

The seven or more years I spent at Elmers Court boarding school weren't all bad. Oh yes, there was the obligatory teacher with an overdosed sense of authority to contend with. Picture, if you can, the schoolteacher from Pink Floyd's 'The Trial' depicted in the British-made film, *The Wall*, and there you have him, Mr X, a bullyboy with a mortarboard and a cane, no less. This man had the world at his feet (well, the school at least). A playground for him to wield his sordid and nasty little games, like a foot soldier from the Third Reich governing his dictatorship over those 'unruly little guttersnipes', as he would refer to us. This man would paddle bash us with a long wooden bat, and make us stand in those dark, reverberating, hollow corridors, frightened and alone for hours on end, accompanied only by our vivid young imaginations to really put the fear of God into us.

This man was an out-and-out bully. Even so, without knowing, he probably taught me a lifelong lesson, and that was to always bully the bully – smash the bullies and anyone championing them to pieces, stand shoulder to shoulder with the weak. And this, my new-found accidental friends, has been my mantra from that day to this.

But like I said, boarding school wasn't all bad – twelve lads in a dormitory with no locks or bars to keep us quarantined away from the girls that resided in the other half of that huge establishment. It was a fascinating place to be, and the grounds were as big as five massive rugby pitches. So, as young boys you can easily imagine that the mischief to be had right there at our fingertips was endless.

The music room, with its creaky floors, was next to the dining room at the back of the main entrance, and there was the big staircase up to the first floor. I was in the main house of the old building in a dorm at the top of the stairs. Our dorm overlooked the back of the building that looked right out onto a mass of fields; fields that ran and ran, leading your eye until you were visibly introduced to the Isle of Wight. Given the mileage, I was actually closer to the Isle of Wight than I was to my parents' home in Hayes. I remember we were not allowed to play on the lawn, and if you were ever caught running across it, well, let's just say you were bang in trouble. You had to walk around the path on the edges.

Like I said, I was in the main house, but I remember the lodges and the multi-storey extension to the left where I think there were girls' dorms as well. *Who am I kidding? I knew exactly where their dorm was!* There was a big hall at the back, an extension block that housed a stage, and I think there was a courtyard with temporary buildings in, which I believe were more classrooms. I remember sitting in those classrooms for the compulsory weekly writing home period. As always, my mind was blank, with not a bloody clue what to write; staring at a blank sheet, hoping letters forming words would drop in from the sky.

One of the most memorable things from my time at Elmers was the morning call to wake us up – a tune that was played out on a set of tubular bells. To be honest, I thought that tubular bells was a made-up instrument for that Oldfield fella's album until the first time I saw them in the main house of our school.

This place was one big playground: a young boy's dream for adventure and exploration. The games you could play, and the villainous behaviours you could get up to, were endless. Oh, and the added promise of showing off this chicanery to the young girls in the adjacent dorm was just like icing on an impressionable young boy's cake. So, in the dead of night, when the hierarchy had taken themselves off to the study rooms for cigars and brandy, my good friend, Michael Byrne, and I, armed with a fresh bout of confidence, slipped through the dorm window and out onto the balcony, shimmying our way across to where the girls were sleeping. Forgetting, in a moment of naivety, that girls can be a little sensitive, we eased ourselves through their window and were immediately met by a profusion of shrieks.

'Oh shit, now we're in big trouble!' we thought, as we tried to laugh through it.

The mayhem that followed as we scampered from the girls' room window in the next five minutes would ensure our immediate capture. As we climbed back through to our own dorm we were met by judge, jury and executioner, or Mr X, as he is more respectfully known. We knew this wasn't going to be easy, because this bully hated the ground we walked on, so it was six of the best for me and my pal, with a booby prize of a five-hour nose-to-the-wall impasse. Oh well, we knew what we were getting into and, with that in mind, we thought, sod it, let's have another go next week. That Michael was a bit of a lunatic, but a fantastic mate to have around.

If nothing else, I am a sucker for punishment. Although, if my memory serves me correctly, I kept my nose clean for a little while because we were coming up to visiting weekend; the time our parents would come up to see us. I certainly did not want to incur the wrath of my dad after finding out that I had been a little troublemaker. It's funny, you know, but as a young lad, I remember gauging the time between visits against the time it would take me to build the model vehicle that my parents had brought for me on their last visit: according to my fine mathematical calculations, I'm guessing that it was around once every six weeks or so.

As they arrived, we would be out on parade, very similar to that of a military one. My pals and I were now a well-oiled machine; buffed and ready for the Gestapo to exhibit to a crowd of expectant parents. Deep down, my dad would have seen right through all of this pomp and circumstance. Dad was old school to the core, having served in the forces, so this would have been old hat to him. Either way, I certainly didn't expect a pat on the back from that direction. Funny how things change as you get older. More recently, on a trip to see my family up north, Dad and I were sat alongside each other and, realising how big and powerful I had got, he pulled me to one side and said, ''Ere, son, I'm sorry. As a father, while you was growing up, I thought that I had been bad to you.'

'Don't be silly, Dad,' I said. 'I respect you as my father. I wouldn't dream of raising my hand to you. I just want you to respect me as your son in the same way that I respect you as my dad.'

In Hayes, in the area where I grew up, there were the obvious bullies. Many of them were a lot bigger than me because as a child, I was small, but even as a skinny young lad, I knew how to throw my hands about a bit. I remember one time, this bully and his pals set upon me and, all of a sudden, I went wild and started to unload, throwing punches into the biggest one. In the blink of an eye there was a crowd forming, and in the mayhem and noise, and because it was right outside our house, my dad had been alerted to it. So, I'm hitting this bully with so many shots he doesn't know what's coming next, and he's coughing and squealing like a pig when all of a sudden, my dad's positive chants cheering me on turned into, 'Stop … stop … stop, son!'

You see, in my anger, I wasn't just hitting the bully, I was also putting some good shots into my dad's car too. That motor was his pride and joy, his best bit of kit, and there was me smashing a granny out of it.

The fight was soon over and the bullies retreated, embarrassed. I'm pleased as punch to be the victor, until I think of the damage I've done to my dad's car and the thought of the hiding I'm going to get as a result of it. However, on this occasion, I didn't get into trouble because Dad must've been proud of me wiping out the bullyboy.

I imagine that sounds a bit like I was terrified of my dad. I guess it seems like my dad would beat us all of the time, but that wasn't the case at all. He did belt us now and again, and I was scared of him a bit, but it was more out of respect. Most of the time my dad only had to give me a look and I knew right there and then that I needed to turn it in and behave myself.

Back in those days even the girls could have a tear up, and I don't mean with another girl, no, I mean with the boys. My sister, Win, was a proper little handful. I remember boys taking the piss out of her in the street and she would just go into them, and she smashed a fair few of them up too, make no mistake about that. To be honest, I think that it was my sister that first encouraged me to use my fists and stick up for myself.

All that said, on occasion I actually came unstuck. This particular tear up happened in my late teens. My cousin Jerry and

I had gone out for a bit of a booze-up, probably to see if we could pull a couple of sorts. Unbeknownst to me at the time, the couple of sorts we had chosen to move in on were accompanied by a local bullyboy, and a big lump of a bullyboy at that. No sooner had we left and were walking away, these three motors pulled up and a bunch of fellas jumped out of each car. Well, this lot put it right on us, smashing us to bits with bats and all sorts. It was a bit naughty because Jerry and I were only a couple of young whippersnappers – all flared jeans and bum fluff. I tried my best, throwing a few shots around, but this one guy was just too big, he looked like Desperate Dan next to Jerry and me. Well, anyway, this lot done a bit of a number on me and smashed my nose right up with a bat, broken and bloodied – it almost ruined my dashing good looks, too!

I went through a fair amount of bullies as I braved my teenage years. Now, I'm not here to make the same old excuses that we've heard a million times, such as, 'I was bullied a lot, so I chose to fight back,' and all that sort of cobblers. No, my story is a little different. You see, believe it or not, I actually didn't set out wanting to have fights, I just did it to get myself out of trouble and, over the years and after many, many brawls, I learned to use the talent that God had given me to my advantage. Now, if that meant that over time I became 'a bit of a tasty git', or 'mustard with me hands', as Lenny McLean would often put it, then I'm afraid that was simply my destiny and the cards that this young boy from Hayes had been dealt – a destiny that has, for the most part, served me very well. Furthermore, this God-given talent had taken me to places I could have only ever dreamt about. Believe me, I learned many valuable lessons growing up through my teenage years that have held me in good stead. It helped me move right up through the ranks, from a skinny little runt with muscles like knots in hankies to a sixty-inch-chested bodybuilder minding some top-drawer names of the era, such as Iron Mike Tyson and a whole heap of others. But I'll tell you about them later.

2
HAPPY IN THE HAYES

I say I was happy in the Hayes, which was true as long as I was
doing my own thing and people were leaving me alone. I have
no idea why, but they always seem to pick on me. I had some
silly idiot acting like a fool, showing off in front of his mates,
changing my surname trying to be smart. Well, he came unstuck for that little piss-take. I think he had had a bit of a tear
up with my brother, Mick, and managed to get the better of
him so, in turn, this boy thought he could do the same to me.
This one particular day he was with his pals, goading me.

'Hooochin, Hoochin,' he was shouting.

'Who the hell are you?' I fired back at him.

'I smashed your fucking brother, now it's your turn.'

With that, I let him have it and unloaded a combination of
punches into him, quick and sharp. I just kept ploughing into
him so that he would think twice about taking the piss out of
me again. I remember thinking, *right, now I've got rid of him,
the rest of them will give me a bit of a wide berth*. But, at home
time as I was leaving school, I spotted this big gang, including
the bully and all of his brothers, waiting for me. I tried to walk

around each one of them, but they were hemming me in, trying to have a go at me. With that, they pinned me to a fence and all set about me, giving me a bit of a hiding.

Immediately after, I made my way to a red phone box and got on the blower to Dave Caves, but his older brother, Les, answered instead. Now, this fella was a right handful. His muscles used to rip through his shirt as he was walking down the local high street. He was tattooed, but very smart, and not your typical seventies Neanderthal heavy that roamed the streets like some unfinished monkey project. No, this fella was a well-groomed, fashionable geezer and that was probably a shock to most people who picked a fight with him because he didn't look one bit like your average raving lunatic. Anyway, he asked me what was wrong, and I told him that I had been attacked by these brothers and their bullying mates, and that was that. Les rounded the boys up and we paid these brothers a visit and smashed the life out of them. Now, you would think that with me being associated with the likes of Les and Dave Caves that people would leave me alone, and although this was the case for a little while after that little fracas, it very soon started again. You can ask anyone that knows me and they will tell you that I am just John, there is no bravado, I don't puff my chest out and go about all leary, looking for trouble. But people have picked fights with me my whole life. Even on the doors at my biggest and most powerful, people just seem to take a dislike to me.

So, the fights were coming in thick and fast at school. On one occasion, everyone made a circle around me and I was more or less bullied into fighting. Like I said, I didn't really want to have a fight, but I'd had enough of being bullied, so I just let loose and unloaded on him. I didn't really know what I was doing, but I came out the victor anyway.

Another day I fought three brothers with my sister there watching. I smashed the first one, then spun the next one round by his jumper and hooked him, and he went down, so I hit the other one, too, for just being with them.

When I was about fifteen or so, I dropped out of school. Well, I say I dropped out, but in actual fact, I was suspended quite a few times for silly things like driving my dirt bike down one of the main corridors. Let's just say that the teachers and staff at Townfield did not take very kindly to me and were probably not that unhappy to see the back of me.

I was already working at a butcher's shop a while before I actually left school. It felt a bit strange at first because it was the same butcher my mum used when I was just a young boy, but I fit in very easy, and I got on great with the lads that worked there, they were a great bunch of fellas.

Being the new boy meant that doing delivery duties on the company boneshaker was seventy per cent of my job description and I absolutely loved it. Moreover, while I had the boneshaker, I could run a few little errands of my own, whizzing off round my aunt's to see my cousin Jerry would be one of my most popular detours, but I never strayed from my path too much. No way did I want to be seen by any of the other butcher's boys. Losing that job at that juncture in my life would have ruined me, so I always kept my nose clean.

I also did a spell with the RAF Air Cadets, and I liked it there. I guess I had grown accustomed to the military way of life from my boarding school days. I learned a lot with the Air Force, and I like to think that it impressed my dad – the idea that I just took it upon myself to join up probably made him feel proud, but I guess I'll never know.

But the bullies kept on coming. One time, as I was walking home through the estate, I spotted some lads huddled in a group. I thought nothing of it at first and just made my way past them, but they had a bucket full of petrol, and as I got past them, one of them doused me with it and another of them threw a lit rag onto me. My leg went up in flames like a bonfire. Panic-stricken, I hurried off around the corner and onto the main high street, where my good pal, Jim, happened to be walking. I shouted out to him, and in seeing my distress, he came running over and quickly began wrapping his coat around me to quell the fire. The flames subsided, but underneath it felt as though I had lava running over my leg, burning into my skin, and I was in complete agony. Anyway, a trip to the hospital to get it looked at was my next move, and they bandaged me up, and I headed home. I still have the scars on my shin as evidence.

That little escapade was over, for me, at least, but those lads ain't getting away with it, I thought, they'll get what they deserve very soon. I bided my time and did a number on every last one of them; all except one who I never managed to track down until I finally spotted him, years later, heading into our local Jobcentre. By this time, I was in excellent shape.

I'd been training and I'd also been learning to box properly. I parked my motorbike up, took my boxing gloves out of the top box, and sat on the wall opposite for a long time. Finally, I saw him heading for the main door, and he was just about to step out when he spotted me. He must have known exactly what was going to happen and so, like the bullyboy does, the coward in him pulled back inside and he sat in there until I left. If I didn't have somewhere else to be, I would have waited all day long until they closed, and he would be forced to come out. But never mind, I thought to myself, every dog has its day.

Funnily enough, I caught up with another bully at the Job-centre a few months later. I'd gone to do a book signing, and this bully who had picked on me years before was sitting at one of the tables. I went up to his desk and sat down, my head bowed so he couldn't see my face.

'Can I help you?'

With that, I lifted my head, looking up slowly, and said, 'You don't remember me, do you?'

At that point, he started to twitch; I could see the colour drain from his face as the realisation of just who I was had come over his boat like a tidal wave.

'I'm John Houchin. Remember what you used to do to me in school?'

By this point, the blood had well and truly disappeared right out of him, and I said, 'Right, I'll be outside when you come out and we can have a chat about them days, settle our differences.'

I immediately stood bolt up and walked out of there like John Wayne with attitude.

When I have a beef to settle, I can be a very patient sort of fella, and this time was no exception because I waited outside. I sat on that same wall opposite for over an hour, slowly watching the place emptying as it was getting close to closing time.

I watched a whole heap of people leave, but there was no sign of the bullyboy; he must have found another way out of the building through an escape exit. However, by this point I'd had enough of everything, and I just wanted to get on in life on whichever path seemed the best for me at that time.

I had always been interested in looking after myself, even while I was acting silly, smoking and drinking, but I knew if I was going to take it seriously, the fags and the odd drink would simply have to go. So, here's where it started: welcome to the new and improved John. Forget the Muscles from Brussels and all that cobblers, there's a new kid on the block. Ladies and gents, be upstanding for the Muscles from Middlesex.

3
FROM KINANE TO McLEAN

So here I am, almost eighteen, and just getting on with things in everyday life. I had decided I was going to toughen up, on account of all the people, for some unknown reason, who were still having a go at me. I'd been in a fight that had nothing to do with me, and had attempted to hold my hands up, but I just did not have enough power. I'd finally had enough – I needed a new game plan.

Being the kind of fella I am – methodical to the core with a little sprinkling of OCD to kick the whole thing up a gear – the next few years of my life were spent trawling the gyms, from Gold's to Del's and back again, on my quest to become the next Lou Ferrigno.

I started on my mission to train like the elite. I would equip myself with a brand spanking new notepad and pencil, and then spend hours just sat watching these people train, and while I watched and studied, I jotted everything down. Once I had filled my brain with what I saw as adequate knowledge, I quickly signed the relevant forms and joined the gym. From that day forward, I would be buying magazines regularly and writing every exercise down. I would even draw diagrams and caption them for training, too. Very quickly, I became obsessed. I was completely in awe of these huge, muscular bodybuilders and it became my passion and my dream to be just like them.

With my newfound knowledge, I guess I was even starting to think like a bodybuilder; I was eating the right foods and getting stronger and stronger by the day. In addition to this, my body was starting to change dramatically. I had developed muscles in places I didn't know existed. As I mentioned previously, I also knew how to swing my arms around in quite a controlled manner, probably because subconsciously, I had picked up a lot of tips while watching the old boxing bouts on TV. Personally, I don't think that I was born a fighter but many others, including my pals, would totally disagree; I believe that I was just useful with my hands. So, with this newfound strength I had recently acquired, I infused both attributes together and created a brand spanking new me.

I met some top-drawer bodybuilders back then, all of whom taught me some invaluable lessons that simply cannot be learned from watching tapes and reading books. No, this was the hands-on kind of experience; the type of private tuition that people today pay an absolute fortune for. While many people gained their morsels of knowledge watching *Pumping Iron*, I gained mine listening to the top scientific bodybuilding specialists of the time from across the pond. I also spent time around the British equivalents and, for this reason alone, my pathway to becoming a competitor was a much shorter journey.

I used to spend a lot of time at Uncle Tony's house. Now, Tony, my dad's brother, was a good boxer; so good, in fact, he once sparred with the Finnegan brothers, and had twice beaten Olympic gold medal winner Chris Finnegan in the past. That gives you an idea of his abilities, so his knowledge, to me, was invaluable.

It's a small world too because my pal, Lenny McLean, used to spar with the brothers up at Freddie Hill's gym around the same sort of time. Uncle Tony was really good to me, and he taught me some moves too. At the time I didn't take it too seriously, but it must have had a lasting effect because those moves came in very handy as I worked my way through those rough pubs and clubs years later. Besides, it just goes to show why many people think that Lenny and I fought similarly with our fists. We had obviously, yet inadvertently, been taught the same old school ways of using 'yer 'ands', as Lenny would put it. Speed and power are paramount. But also, never let the one you're going up against you know what, or when, it's coming.

One day this fella called Mick Kinane brought his son, Blue, with him to train at the Brunel gym, and very quickly, I got to know the pair of them quite well. While chatting one day, Mick happened to mention that he worked security on the doors. At that time, I think that Mick was in his late forties, so he was obviously a very seasoned bouncer through experience alone. He had a day job though, too, which was his own company, Speedway Farm – something to do with haulage and logistics. Mick was a very sharp fella – he rented a bit of land to keep a pair of horses on, then he bought it for a few quid, and, over time, it grew into a small fortune.

Mick had a heavy reputation and, by all accounts, was a well-respected fighting force on the manor. I was young at the time and didn't have a clue who he was, but Mick must have seen something special in me because he would always compliment me on my progress and training regime, which boosted my confidence tenfold.

Soon after getting to know Mick and Blue, I was entrusted with his address and so started popping round to his house for a cuppa and a chat. Mick then started taking me to all these places where he was running the doors and I started to notice that wherever Mick went, he would get special treatment – free drinks, food, anything; he was treated like royalty. We would often go to one of his clubs called Tudors.

'Sort John out a nice roast dinner and whatever else he wants to drink please, ladies?' he would say to the staff.

We spent hours in these places, then when it was time to leave, Mick would hand me a wedge of dough and he'd say, 'There you go, son, a nice little few quid for ya!'

I just used to look into my hand in astonishment as Mick walked off, thinking, what has he given me all of this money for? I was only a young fella at the time, and I told myself that he was just helping me out with a bit of cash. Looking back now, it was obvious what he was paying me for. He knew that if a bit of trouble had kicked off, I would have been straight in there to watch his back.

Not too long after we started socialising together, Mick said to me, 'I've got a bit of door work for you, John.'

He took me along to one of his clubs, where I sat patiently until I saw any sign that there was going to be a bit of trouble, at which point, I'd follow him in. By this time in our friendship, he knew that I was a bit tasty with my fists.

'If it goes off, John, just stay with me and watch my back.'

Many times, after gym sessions, I would go back with Mick to his house for a cuppa. Mick's lovely wife, Val, was often at home, getting ready to go off to work. I had been spending so much time around Mick's house that Val had become like a second mum to me. Mick was always on the lookout for an opener for a bit of graft so he said, 'Here, Val, see if there's any work going at your place for John, will you?'

And lo and behold, she got me a bit of work down the pub where she was working. So, there I was, getting thirty-five notes a shift, along with a nice meal, and all this for just sitting there in much the same way as I had done with Mick at Tudors. If it did go off, I would quickly steam in and sort it, but most of the time it was quite relaxed, and I didn't have to do a great deal.

After about a year or so, I moved to a lively and rough old place. I was working with two top fellas, Sid McFarlan and

John Crossen, and another useful doorman that they called Popeye, or just Pops for short. Now this place was bloody brutal. There would be fighting every night of the week; glasses were being smashed all over the shop, it was like a scene from that *Roadhouse* movie with Patrick Swayze, with people being hurled over the bar.

There was an incident in the men's toilets one night, and I had to bash the door down to get involved. Sid, who was a right handful, was on top of this fella and it looked like he was about to kill him. I had no choice but to get myself in among it and pull Sid off this geezer because I guarantee, if I didn't, Sid would have ended up doing prison. I say that because the fella that Sid was bashing up was already smashed to bits when I turned up. When it had all calmed down, I noticed that Sid had lined bottles up ready to smash this fella with, so it's safe to say that he was pretty lucky I was there.

Another good doorman who worked there with me was a fella called Paul. Now, Paul knew that I was only a young lad starting out and would often say to me, 'Make sure I'm here with you before going into fights, OK, John?'

They didn't come much better than my dear pal, Paul O'Loughlin. He was second to none, this fella, and a top bloke too. Over the years, I spent a great deal of time with him, and he taught me so much. I remember him telling me that if I was minding a door and it came on top, so much so that I was fighting for my life and there seemed to be no help coming, then I should do whatever necessary just to get the job done.

In other words, anything goes. 'Tables, chairs, knives, anything!' Paul said. 'If you can't grab hold of anything else, even sling the bloody landlord at 'em!'

To be quite honest, yet not meaning to give myself a gee, it usually only took me one shot to put them away. By that time in my life, I had built up so much speed and had gotten that powerful, that was all it took. Nine times out of ten, a good left-hander would usually do the trick and finish a row before it had started. Some people used to come back a week or so later after I'd hit them, not to have another go, oh no, they'd come back to apologise – even after a week or more, they'd still be in a bit of a mess. I used to think to myself, bloody hell, John, did you really do that to him?

If I'm in a row then I know it's all just down to me and my two fists. I didn't need marching powder (cocaine) to get the job done; I have never taken it, that never interested me one bit. Drugs are for mugs is my motto! All I needed was my fists and pure adrenaline, and I got the job done very well on that God-given commodity.

Mick was also running the doors at another place called Melanie's, and he got me a weekend job there. No sooner had I started, and I'd been forced to smash this bunch of fellas up, good and proper.

'Fucking hell, John, mate. I only put you in there for the weekend and you're smashing every fucker to pieces!' he said.

'Mick,' I replied, 'I hit one guy over the table, and he landed on the guvnor of the pub's missus, who nearly flew onto the floor. These men came down looking for a fight, Mick, they were goading me! Anyway, with that, the guvnor came steaming over, pointing at me, shouting, "I don't want him here. He's a raving fucking lunatic, he's nearly killed my missus for fuck's sake."'

Mick's hands were tied.

'I'll put you somewhere else for a little while, John, just while it cools down a bit, alright, son?'

Before I even met Lenny McLean, it turns out that Mick Kinane and he had had a bit of a run-in when working the doors at Camden Palace. Mick told me the story and was saying to me that he found Lenny a bit strange the first night he worked with him. What had happened was Mick had been called in to work because they were a man down and, as luck would have it, Mick fancied a change of scenery so agreed to help them out.

Now, whether it was because Mick was new or not was a mystery to him, but he said that Lenny just seemed to look at him as if he was a piece of shit, a nobody. This all felt a bit strange because Mick was very well known among the heads of the underworld, not to mention that his nickname was Mad Nick at the time. Mick said that he thought Lenny knew exactly who he was, but was just weighing him up, and that was why he was being a little standoffish. Later in the evening, some lunatic kicked off and, within a split-second,

Mick had grabbed him around the throat, pinched a pressure point and the man collapsed to the floor. This changed Lenny's mood a little because for the rest of the night he just looked Mick up and down in a way that suggested that he could not believe what he had just seen. The speed and ease with which Mick had dealt with this idiot had obviously impressed Len, greatly.

The following night, Mick was back on the door. He acknowledged everyone with a nod and a wink. When it came to Lenny, much to his surprise, there seemed to be an air of respect coming Mick's way and Len said, ''Ere, Mick, you're alright you are, mate. It's good to have you as part of our team.'

Years later, on a visit back to Middlesex to see my pal, Mick, he heard I was working with Len and said, 'Look, John, don't go down the road of trying to be the hardest man in the world. Just be yourself, like you have always been when you were with me.' He said, 'Listen, son, there are some tough men out there, and they're waiting around every corner, so just be alert and aware, all of the time.'

I think he was trying to say do not go looking for a reputation, which I never did. Mick knew I was not a silly boy, he knew that I would take his every word on board.

Mick taught me a lot while I was under his wing. He was not the biggest fella on the planet, although he was six foot and had hands like shovels and be sure he could hit with them. The martial arts study and training that he had adopted over the years certainly helped him a lot. Mick knew how to take legs out with one quick snap, and his Spock-like death grips on a troublemaker's pressure points were second to none – most attackers would go to sleep in a flash with a single one, and when they were coming round, unaware of what had just happened, Mick would say something like, 'Are you alright, son? You must have fallen and bumped your head.' Those idiots would just agree and go about their business.

I remember one night we walked into Tudors, and this gigantic fella was causing a bit of grief with the bar staff. Mick said to me, 'Hold up, John, I'll sort this out,' and with that, he walked over nonchalantly, signalled for the man to drop down to his level so that he could whisper in his ear and while he was hunched down low, bang! Mick hit him with a thundering right-hander. The fella immediately shot back, bolt upright on his legs, and then dropped like a fallen oak tree – he was out cold. Due to the size of the man, it took about five bouncers to lift him and get him out of the place.

A few days later, we're stood at the bar. Mick was propped up, smoking his pipe like a noble country gent, when the colossal fella that he had dropped walked through the door.

Mick says, 'Hold up, fellas, look whose just came in.'

The big fella then walks over to Mick, apologises, and shakes his hand while saying to the bar staff, 'Whatever this man and his pal are drinking is all on me. I'm sorry for my antics the other night.' Then he said to Mick, 'I have never been knocked out in my life, what did you hit me with?'

To which Mick replied, 'Just my fist, son. Just a simple right-hander.' And that, my friends, was that.

During the years I spent with Mick and his boys we did a lot of damage to a lot of people but, mark my words, these were people who were looking for it – known troublemakers – and we, as bouncers, were simply defending ourselves. Mick would often say to me, 'Don't go rushing in, John. Get in close and tight to them and, with a whisper, not a growl, let them know the score.' Mick's subtle and unassuming technique worked like a treat, but on the odd occasion that it didn't, a quick bang to the chin would usually sort it.

One New Year's Eve night, while I was still working at another rough house, it went off proper – the only way I can explain it was a mini massacre – it felt like we were fighting for our lives. There were glasses smashed all over the shop, blood everywhere; people were walking around like a bomb had just gone off.

In the end, the Old Bill arrived and there were police dogs everywhere. The riot squad had been ordered down and, in about ten minutes flat, there were tons of people arrested. A few days following, I was down the gym training with my pal Harry, or H, as he was known, and he said, 'Sack off working all of these rough houses, John, and come and work with us full-time.'

Within no time at all, I was commuting to work with H and his boys in the West End, which was a bit more upmarket and there were far fewer tear ups for the pound note. I still stayed in touch with Mick because he had been like a father figure to me, but it was time to turn the page to the next footprint on my journey. This was a footprint of considerable strength and merit, with a dash of lunacy added into the bargain, and they don't come more powerful than the next fella Mick introduced me to.

4
THE HOSTESS WITH THE MOSTESS

It was getting a bit tedious, toing and froing on a forty-five-minute trek from job to job; it was starting to do me in. Nevertheless, peeking over the London horizon, a change for the better was imminent. While working a club around 1987, called Ferdenzie's, I met a particular person who was very quickly about to change my life. This beautiful lady, inside out, turned out to be my soul mate, Dana Sealy. Dana was a model, and she worked at many of the finest and most classy gentlemen's establishments in London Town, and Michael Ferdenzie's club was of exactly that calibre.

I remember the first time she caught my eye. I was mesmerised, as I'm sure a great many of you would be, too. She's in the club, and I'm trying my very best to get her attention. I'm making all of the usual flirty motions a fella of my size has the ability to do. After a short while I catch her, she's facing the mirror, I point at her in the reflection and sort of beckon her to me, like a Mills & Boon love story this for those of you old enough to remember them. My advances have been noticed, and Dana comes over. I try with the usual patter, but Dana is old school, this ain't going to cut any ice. Fuck it, I'll just be myself, I thought, and from that moment on, we became the very best of friends. After a short courting period, I said to Dana, 'Listen, I'm living in Hayes and you're in Tooting – it's a bit of a hike. How do you fancy living together?' She said, 'Yeah, go on then. I suppose I've grown a little fond of you now, John-John!' Followed by hysterical laughter, and, within the week, I had moved in with her, and thought to myself, 'Right, son, this is it, you're home.'

Living in south London in the late eighties, we had the usual ups and downs. I remember Dana having murders (trouble) from the tenant downstairs – this woman was an absolute nightmare. Dana had mentioned her and the trouble she had brought to Dana's door a few times while we were in our dating period. I remember thinking, bloody hell, that would tip me over the edge, that would, and one day it did. I was in bed, stark bollock naked, when the troublemaker from downstairs' fella has appeared at our door, doing his nut about my boy, James. I'd heard enough and leapt out of bed, and while remembering to hide my modesty with a t-shirt, I ran over to the door, and *bang!* I put a left hook into him, and he's flown down the stairs at speed.

'Next time you want to borrow a cup of sugar, ask a bit more politely, yeah?' I hollered down to him. He must have taken umbrage to that because he never darkened my door again.

Like I said, there was only ever the odd bit of grief; most of the time spent with my little family was pure bliss. I do remember getting into it with Dana one night, though. James was staying out at his aunt's, and I came home with a bit of an attitude and it erupted. Dana went completely off her nut – well, this was the very last time I had a battle with her. She turned into a woman possessed, and I really do mean that. She was chasing me around the bedroom with a chopper, and by that, I don't mean a seventies two-wheeler, oh no, I mean an actual bloody *axe*!

Listen, I have been in some rucks in my life, but being chased by a woman with the hump, wielding a chopper, took it to another level. I mean, let's get this right, there's nothing you can do in a situation like that. If it were a man, I'd have just knocked him spark out, but I have never laid a hand on a woman before and never, ever would. Which is a good job too, because by her reaction I had just witnessed while we were having our little barny, I guarantee that the chopper would've been planted in my head. All I could do was take hold of her and sit her on the bed to calm her down. However, and like I said earlier, ninety per cent of the time our little family home life was harmonious, we had some absolutely fantastic times.

In our house we were always fooling around. Dana used to watch on from the door as James and I made breakfast with towels on our heads. James was always laughing, and that meant that my boy was a guaranteed audience for me showcasing my inner clown.

I remember some kid around the corner pinching James's bike one day; I was at work at the time, but when I arrived home, Dana told me, and I tore around there to see the kid's parents. Unfortunately, it wasn't the amicable handover I'd initially hoped for, no. This fella and his brother got a bit leary and, for that, they had to be introduced to a swift backhander, one quick belt on the chin and it was all over. The fella's brother immediately started pleading with me not to give him the same, so I didn't touch him. I mean, come on, I'm no bully: if a man backs down, I consider him to be weaker than me and won't lay a finger on him. Anyhow, the job was done. James was happy again, cycling around the streets like a lunatic with his pals, and the man's son never stole a thing from James ever again. Dana said, 'John-John, I think your little chat did the trick!' Dana never asked questions, she just let me do what I did best, but if I was going to do something that was way off the mark, she would certainly not have hesitated to air her concerns. Thankfully, that was never really on the cards as I always tried to stay out of trouble and keep the peace.

I said we had a harmonious existence and now I'm going to moan again – well, I have to, it was my life, and there is no getting away from that. I pulled up outside our house one day and there's a private cab in my parking space with his motor running. Anyway, I give him a little toot on my horn to let him know I'm there, but he ignores it. Right, I'm thinking, I'll toot a little harder then and, hopefully, he'll liven himself up and move along. Still nothing! OK, this silly idiot is starting to be a bit leary, so I jumped out of my car and made my way over to him.

'Here, mate, did you not hear me tooting for you to move up a bit? I'm trying to get parked on my front!'

With that, he goes, 'Fuck off, I'm not going anywhere, pal!'

Right, that's done it! This cheeky sod has had enough warnings – it's time for a stiff talking-to.

Immediately, I went to work. Dragging him from his motor, I gave him a left hook and he flew up in the air and landed on his bonnet. I grabbed hold of him and smashed into him a bit more for taking a bloody liberty, and all this time my missus, Dana, is hanging out the window, screaming and hollering at me, 'Get off him, John, leave him alone.'

He was only there to pick her up and take her to work, but I didn't have a clue. Anyway, with that, I've livened myself up and ran off down the road. I didn't want to hang about because I could bet a pound to a penny that somebody would most definitely have phoned the Old Bill, so I had it away on my toes down the road and made my way to my pal's video shop. Hurtling through his door, I'm shouting, 'I've just done a cabby for getting a bit leary. I'll have to lay a bit low in your stock cupboard for a bit, Frankie boy.'

Frank then says, 'You think the Old Bill are coming for you, mate?'

To which I replied while laughing, 'Nah, sod the Old Bill! It's Dana I'm worried about, mate.'

Frank and I had a few coffees and a chat about the mouthy cabby, and then I did the Walk of Shame home. Well, after Dana read me the riot act, and after she had done her nut for the best part of seven hours, she told me that about ten cabs turned up after I had had it away. She then said that as soon as they had seen the number of our place and realised it was me that lived there, they all cleared off.

Another time, I remember some lowlife trying to bully someone, and I had no choice but to step in. You see, there was this fella – a good friend of Dana's – who had fairly severe learning difficulties. Anyway, what happened was that he had gone to this local furniture shop to purchase a sofa, and the bullying bloke that owned the shop had taken advantage of his disability and sold him a second-rate pile of shit. It was a total bunch of junk; in fact, it broke as soon as this fella got it home. So, Dana has got on the blower to me and given me the SP (information), so I obviously told her to leave it with me to sort out.

Later that day, I made my way round to the shop to give the owner a lesson in retail therapy. I walked in, and he was there, giving it large to a couple, trying to do them out of a few bob, no doubt. I waited until they had left and then I said, 'Here, listen, I want a word with you.' I told him what I'd seen him do, and what I now wanted him to do, and he started getting a bit leary, so I've knocked him spark out onto one of his sofas. I thought to myself, he can have a little sleep there, and when he wakes up, he will have realised the error of his ways and make things right with the friend of Dana's that he's tried to mug off. Funnily enough, Dana's friend ended up with a sofa three times more expensive than the one he had initially bought. Oh, and Dana was gifted with a beautiful new cabinet that she'd had her eye on for a while – result!

*

We often visited my parents in Hayes and a few times a year my mum would invite us over for a Sunday roast. The thing is, my mum wasn't the best of cooks and I have always been a bit picky with food, so that combination could end up being a right disaster. What would always happen was we would go over for dinner and then Dana, me and James would stop off at The Ritz for a proper meal afterwards.

I was very fortunate with my love of fine cuisine, because having a lady like Dana made that easy. She was a fantastic cook, and very well educated in foods from around the globe. Mind you, I bet I drove her mad at times with my menu demands while I was on season (in training) – I must have been a blinking nightmare.

However, no challenge was too much for Dana, and she cooked the most exceptional foods, particularly her Guyanese cuisine. Her mantra was 'the way to a man's heart is through his stomach', which, in my case, could not be more accurate. My bodybuilding regime was specific, and Dana was the perfect supplier, so, I'd often eat us out of house and home. I do think she found it a massive task, keeping up with the number of chickens I consumed, but she certainly managed it – that lady fed my boy James and me like royalty.

And at that time I really needed it. I had moved up the ranks, my name was getting around, and I would soon end up shoulder to shoulder with the legendary streetfighter and King of the Bouncers, Lenny 'The Guv'nor' McLean.

5
THIS BOY'S MUSTARD

The very first time I met Lenny McLean was in the mid-eighties at the Camden Palace – the very same venue where Mick Kinane had first met him on the doors. Lenny was looking after the place, and we met through mutual friends of ours, Flat-nose Carl, and one of my closest friends from back then, and still today, Al Crossley. Carl and I used to work the doors together. He was also an unlicenced boxing promoter and worked for a London outfit called Bulldog Promotions. Readers may remember Carl standing with his back to the camera in the changing room at Woodford Town Football Club minutes before the Lenny vs Man Mountain York fight. Carl is the man saying to Len, 'I'm keen, I'm mean, I'm Lenny McLean.'

Once Lenny knew me properly, he told me that he'd heard a lot about me from Crossley and Carl. My friendship with those two men went back quite a long way, and like I said, Carl used to arrange the odd underground fight for the pair of us as well. Carl was the sort of fella who would try and test you. Not in a bad way, or to see you get hurt, he just liked to test you. He would throw up top fighters one after the other to fight me. However, each and every one of them I smashed to pieces and beat in quick time. Lenny said that Carl had told him I was a force to be reckoned with, saying that I could beat any man he put in front of me. Now I thought that saying such a thing to Lenny could quite easily be taken as some sort of challenge, but Len was too smart for that, and he whispered to me one day.

'Don't you worry, son. I've got Carl's fucking number!'

And from that day forward, a fantastic friendship began to bloom between the two of us.

From the very first moment Lenny and I met, I sensed that he had taken to me, and very soon this encounter would lead to me working alongside him at the Hippodrome in Leicester Square. We worked a few doors together and also did other bits of work, such as debt collecting and enforcing – jobs that required muscle to settle people's problems. Lenny would say that he took me under his wing, which is a statement that carried a hell of a lot more weight than anyone could ever imagine.

So, here I am again, moving up the ranks, an up-and-coming name in and around London's underworld with the good fortune of working with two of London's finest bouncers, minders and enforcers: Crossley and McLean. Lenny could see from the off that I was game and that I certainly would not shy away from any trouble that went off, no matter how heavy it got. Whenever it went boss-eyed, I would steam into all kinds of terrifying tear ups and, as soon as the dust settled, Lenny would say, 'You've done mustard there, me'son. I'm proud of you.'

I have always been one to listen and take on board any tips, especially from the best, and I remember Lenny telling me, 'John, always be smart, be quick, and always talk nice to people. But above all, don't be a bully.'

Lenny hated bullies, which I think stemmed from the various beatings he had taken at the hands of his evil stepfather when he was just a boy. He never really spoke much about his upbringing to me. I honestly think he did not want anyone thinking negatively of his mum, in the opinion that she should have maybe done something to stop that bully, Jim Irwin.

Lenny was particular about a number of things, one of them being the gear you wore, especially while working, and would often say to me while checking over my clobber, 'Always wear something baggy, John, 'cos if you can't throw a right-hander like this … ' at which point he would throw a flurry of fast, powerful shadow boxing style shots, ' … if you're all tight and can't move your arms about quick, you won't be able to do anything!'

Lenny was always dressed and ready, to the extent that he used to wear something on his shoes to stop him slipping. He would always say to me, while doing a demonstration, 'Before taking that first shot, plant yourself right into the pavement, John, because the first shot you throw means the most.' I'd wind him up a bit and say, 'What do you mean, Len, like I'm playing golf, teeing off?'

'I'm serious, John,' he'd say, 'just smash 'em big with the first shot, and who knows what next.'

I guess that Lenny saw our work uniform as some sort of battle dress. I would always take what he said on board, what with Lenny being who he was and head doorman. It was this sort of attention to detail that kept him at the top of his game.

During my time spent with Lenny, I have a million different stories to tell. Over the years, people had pressed me heavily to elaborate on various things, saying, can you remember when you did this, and could I remember some pinnacle event that had happened, to which I would often say, 'Remember, I spent over ten years in Lenny McLean's company so for me to put it all into some sort of chronological timeline would be impossible.'

However, it is now time for me to delve into my innermost thoughts and pull as much information as I possibly can from the depths of my subconscious. So, while I steadily oil the cogs of my brain, I'll ease you in gently.

I had now earned the nickname 'The Neck', which came about due to my neck measuring almost twenty-three inches in circumference. I was, and still am, quite happy to have this nickname for the simple reason that many people over the years have struggled to pronounce my surname, and Lenny was no exception. There was I, standing on the door of the Hippodrome, when Lenny says, 'Go on, son, your last name, say it to me again.'

'Well, Len, it's the same as how you say house, with chin on the end, like how-chin.' I replied.

'Oh, fuck all of that cobblers, let's just stick with John the Neck!'

Lenny, of course, thought it was hilarious and would say it over again to the other bouncers on the door. He liked to laugh at his own jokes, did Len. Mind you, most people laughed along with him, no matter how bad they were.

Lenny was a big joker, always playing tricks on people in the clubs. Sometimes, as we were stood on the door at the Hippodrome, he would say, 'Here, John, watch this, son,' and with that, he would bend down and pull the massive rug from under the new doorman's feet; the fella would be on his back, holding his face that he'd smashed with his own hands as he fell to the ground. The pair of us would be crying laughing as the man would jump to his feet, shouting, 'For fuck's sake, what happened? What happened?'

Lenny and I would just be stood there, pissing ourselves laughing, as if we didn't have a clue what he was talking about. He never stopped with the fooling around. Another time, there must have been two hundred people queuing to get into the Hippodrome, and all of the management was stood there as well, and out of the blue, Len would say to me, 'Come on, John, let's practise our lines.'

'But Len, two hundred people are waiting to come inside the club,' I'd jokingly reply, playing along.

'Oh, don't fucking worry about that lot for a minute, John,' he would say, getting into character. Then he'd spin around, walk off, and immediately turn on his Cuban heels and walk towards me, as if approaching for the first time. There would be me, stood straight up as if I was minding some club, and Lenny would go, 'Alright me'son?'

''Ere, that ain't even in the script, Len,' I replied, and immediately, he'd start laughing and say, 'Yeah, I know it ain't, boy, I'm just geeing you up, saying, "Alright me'son".'

During this 'rehearsal', the management are looking over, wondering how long this is going to go on for, but obviously, not one of them had the bottle to say anything to Len. This jovial character was a side of Len that he mostly kept hidden away from the public gaze, but once he allowed you in, you'd find he was just an out-and-out comic. I am telling you now, when Lenny McLean was in a funny mood, rolling off his witty wordplay, he could quite easily have been a stand-up comedian.

The Hippodrome was a tourist place and most of the time you could make light work of it, but every now and again it could get a bit naughty. One night, something had gone off inside the club and murders were going on over the radio. Suddenly, from inside the reception area, there was a voice shouting for Lenny.

'Right, John, jump in the motor, son,' he would say.

Anyone standing close by would be looking bemused, and you could tell they were thinking, jump in what bloody motor? You see, Lenny had his own very individual way of saying things. What he meant was that it was time to go to work. Now, in the 'driver's seat' and always in charge on the way to any trouble would be Lenny himself, with me riding shotgun – his wingman, so to speak. The way I looked at it was that I'd earned my stripes by coming up with the goods every time because, let's face it, you had to be mustard to back up The Guv'nor, 'cos it was no easy task.

One night we were minding this rowdy little drinker when a firm turned up, fancying themselves for some sort of title. There were about fifteen of them altogether, and whether they were tasty fighters or not didn't really make much difference to us, especially with those kinds of numbers – you had to have your wits about you.

With that, Len's gone, 'Jump in the motor, son,' so I'm ready for whatever's coming. Quickly and powerfully, Lenny moved into this bunch head-on, so I've flanked them to mop up any others that may jump in, and we're both unloading shots into each and every last one of these silly idiots. Now, most of them are boozed-up so their bark is far worse than their bite and they're dropping like flies. One of them tried to put a glass into Lenny; I've immediately clocked this and backhanded his own hand, and he's done himself in the nut with it. After a bit of a smash-up, those lunatics are all done, and most of them have run off, leaving the three instigators slumped in the doorway, at which point Len says, 'Right, come on, boy, let's go and get a nice cuppa.' Then he turned to the rest of our team and shouted, 'Get these no-value cunts out of my club!'

There was always some lunatic playing up, making a nuisance of themselves. I remember a time when a handful of lads were giving the bar staff some grief. Lenny rushed his way through the punters and, as we arrived where the trouble was, one of these men started getting lippy, giving it the big one to Lenny. In a split second, Lenny turned and smashed him to the ground while picking another one up by his throat. I gave one of them a little dig and took the wind out of him, and they're all lying there in a heap on the floor, unconscious. Anyway, we put them outside when suddenly they turned back and decided to have a go at us so, just like something out of a cartoon, Len smashed one with a left hook and the other with a straight right to his throat as I unloaded the other one, and the three of them, once again, are knocked out cold on the floor.

'Good work me'son!' Lenny said. ''Ere do the bin men come tomorrow?'

'Yes, Len, of course they do, it's Thursday,' I replied.

'Beautiful! Throw their bodies in the skip and leave them out for the rubbish.'

So, there's me down the back alley, humping these three men into the big yellow skip when Lenny says to me, 'For fuck's sake, John, mind their heads, you might hurt 'em!'

'Mind their bloody heads, Len?' I shout back. 'You weren't saying that just now when you took his head off.' At this point, I spotted one of them twitching. 'Here, Len, one of these silly idiots has started to come around and he's trying to drag himself out of the bin. Shall I phone for a cab 'cos it looks like a trip to hospital is in order to revive him?'

Lenny was laughing as he made his way back to the office for his regular cup of tea.

Another night on the door we were talking. I'd had a bit of trouble with this idiot, and Len said to me, 'Sometimes, John, instead of giving someone a hook, hit them with an open-handed slap.'

'Yeah, but I'm quite powerful, Len,' I replied.

'Yeah, I know you are, son, but let's just have it that, in this instance, he only deserves a bit of a slap.'

With that, he started giving me another demonstration, bending over with his hand almost touching the floor.

'When you give it to him, do it from down here, and come up fast, John.'

'Bloody hell, Len. If I pull my hand that far back, there'll be nothing left of him. That sort of slap would hardly be any different to me giving him a left hook.'

And, while laughing, Len replied, 'Yeah, but knocking someone out with a slap sounds a lot fucking better, don't it, me'son?'

Having known Lenny for quite a while, I started getting used to some of his sayings, so much so that a few of them even stuck. If you go on YouTube and see some interview footage of him, he would say, 'Well, I unloaded the lot of 'em, killed 'em all stone dead!'

Obviously, they weren't really dead, but Lenny just liked how it sounded when he said it.

I remember watching Len on *The Ruby Wax Show*, telling the same story about how he killed them all stone dead, and me and my mate would be laughing our heads off, thinking about it. Another saying he had was, 'I am going to break their jaws!'

Now, he didn't mean it all the time – again, it was just a saying, but sometimes it would turn out to be true. You see, Len was good at reading body language. If people started moving their shoulders, it was a sign that they were about to do something. So, Len wouldn't waste any time: he would just hit them, BANG, straight on the button. On the other hand, if Len knew they weren't even worth a slap, he would just whisper to them quietly, 'Now fuck off before I break ya' jaw!' And that usually had the desired effect. Lenny's dialogue was always quite unique – Guy Ritchie was inspired by many of Len's phrases for his *Lock, Stock* script.

A debt had come in, so Len, Al and I were on our way to collect it. It was a massive amount of dough, Len informed me as we were jumping in the motor. Lenny then gave me the full sp (detail) on the way to the job; telling me that this fella was proper vicious and nasty, so I'd need to have my wits about me. For Len to say that, I knew that I might have my work cut out on this occasion.

'Right, get in gear, son, we're going to go to work,' Lenny said to me.

Now, as my pals will tell you, I'm usually the quiet-looking lunatic type of a guy who doesn't do much talking, the kind of fella who just stares into space as if I'm ready to explode, but I can't help thinking to myself that I hope I do a good job while Lenny and Al are watching me.

When we arrive at the location, I'm at the door with Len and Al behind me when Lenny says, 'Give that door a bit of a boot, son. Let him know we're here.' And as I pulled my foot back, the door swung open. Before I could say a word, the fella at the door said, 'Oh, wait one second,' and he grabbed a pile of cash and handed it to me without a hint of menace. Then he turned around, went inside and shut the door behind him. As we're walking away, I turned to Len and he's got this big grin on his face, laughing, and he says, 'Well, I had to make sure you cut the muster, boy.' And off he skipped, singing and laughing. I'm laughing to myself now, thinking about it, but at the time I thought, you won't get me with that one again, McLean, I'll be ready for you next time. Anyway, that was a nice bit of dough for half an hour's work, and onto the next one we went.

Lenny said to me once, 'John, me ol' son, I'm not really a lion, you know. I make out that I am when I go out of this door because people think I'm not frightened of anything. But that's silly, of course I am. To be honest, it's fear that made me the fighter I am today.' And thinking about it, if you're fighting a good fighter, you need the old butterflies – adrenaline!

Some nights when we were working in the Hippodrome, me and Lenny would be across the road in a little cafe opposite and people would always say, 'If you're minding the Hippodrome, why would you be parked up across the street in a cafe?' Well, the answer is straightforward. You see, if we were needed for anything, one of the doormen from the club would run across and shout for one of us, and we'd be over that road like a bullet out of a gun. We were always either in there or in the reception office just off the side of the main corridor, eating Chinese food or just relaxing with a coffee. Len loved a prawn ball and a bit of chow mein. It's funny to think about the time I spent on various doors with Len because I can honestly say, as doormen, we hardly ever stood on the main door of anywhere because we just didn't have to. Around that time, up and down London, Lenny's name was deterrent enough and very quickly, my name had a certain amount of weight in that direction too. Lenny used to say to me, 'Look, John, we don't need to be stood on that door because all we need to know is that if there's any trouble we'll go in and sort it out.' And when trouble did arise, that's precisely what would happen. Then we would go and have a nice cup of tea.

There was one night, for example, when we had just had this smash-up with a bunch of silly idiots. We had gone back to the office to calm ourselves down a bit, because we're still buzzing with adrenaline. Anyway, we're sat in there after this row and without announcing himself, the manager comes barging in through one of the doors. Now, you have to remember that we are still wound up a bit. Lenny grabbed him with force and threw him straight out through the other door – it was so fast, all in a matter of a split second. What had happened was Lenny thought someone was running back in to start trouble again and he had reacted straight away; you see, you had to be on your guard at all times. Lenny always had that ready-to-go at any time way about him, and he instilled the same attitude in me. I don't know if it was from past events, but whatever the reason, he was always very wary and jumpy.

In recent years, a load more information has come out about Len's past concerning his mental state, so maybe the dangerous job we were doing had had an effect on him somewhere along the line. After the incident in the office with the manager, Lenny said to him, laughing, "'Ere, sorry, son, I didn't realise it was you. Now come and sit on Uncle Lenny's knee.' Len grabbed hold of him and bounced him up and down on his knee like one of those puppets you see on the telly. Suffice to say, from that day on, the manager always knocked on Len's office door before entering.

As you would expect, because of Lenny's reputation and notoriety, a significant number of well-known faces would show their faces up the club. Most weekends there would be TV stars, boxers, pundits and radio DJs. Moreover, many faces from *Gangland Britain* would make an appearance, too. A lot of these gangsters might not admit it, but they looked at Lenny like some sort of celebrity.

At this point in his life, Lenny had done quite a lot of TV interviews, and he'd also been on the hit show *The Knock*, which had taken off massively. He also appeared on a documentary with Dave Courtney, for which, I might add, Dave had to pay Len two 'bags o' sand' (a thousand pounds) for the privilege.

'Not bad, eh, John, for a few hours talking about fighting?' Lenny loved a pound note, and by that time in his life, Len was sick of doing favours for people gratis.

***

It had been a quiet night at the Hippodrome and I was on my own, just minding my business at the front door, when Roy 'Pretty Boy' Shaw turned up. Roy was a boxer and had fast become Len's nemesis. I could tell that he had had a few to drink and he was proper wired; he was twitching looking me up down, saying, 'Where is he?'

'Who's that, Roy?' I asked.

'You know who I'm talking about. McLean! Where is he, is he about?'

I thought to myself, oh, here we go, he's going to start. I obviously knew he was talking about Lenny, who by the way was sitting in the office eating some Chinese food, but I certainly wasn't going to tell him that. Roy had a few hangers-on with him who, if I'm honest, looked like they'd been winding him up to cause trouble.

All of a sudden, Roy moved right up into my face with his menacing eyes; not to sound disrespectful but it was clear to see why he had been sectioned in the past. He mumbled at first and then said to me something like, 'It's best you move out the way, because we're coming in the club, no matter what!'

Forever the consummate professional, I said to him, 'Sorry, but I can't do that, Roy, it's more than my job's worth.'

Now, I might have totally got it wrong, and he may have just been after free entry or something, but I simply wasn't prepared to take that chance. By this point, he was almost frothing at the mouth like some rabid Rottweiler, snarling and coming towards me in a threatening manner. I managed to keep my cool, however, because I knew very well that the next onslaught from him could easily be physical and, if that were the case, I would definitely have to trade punches with him. I was already working it out in my head exactly what I was going to do next, so I raised my voice ever so slightly and said, 'Look, Roy, he's around here somewhere, but he's busy with the manager.' Thankfully, that was enough, and he was off on his way down the Charing Cross Road.

I left it a while before going into the office to tell Len, but when I finally got in there I said, 'You won't believe who was outside earlier, Len?'

'Who's that, John?' he enquired.

'It was Shawry, Len,' I said, and his eyes lit up a little.

'You what, son? That fucking Roy down my club?'

'Yeah, Len. Now don't go off your nut, let me explain.'

I began explaining everything as nicely as I possibly could, but Lenny was less than happy that I hadn't called him out front, although he was pleased with the way I had dealt with his arch-enemy.

A few months later, Roy Shaw had gone on some TV programme, challenging Lenny for a return fight. I could see steam coming out of Lenny's ears, and the veins coming up on his neck – he was like a raging bull. I told him to calm down a bit, and said, 'What you going to do, Len, keep fighting him until you're a hundred years old? And with that, he calmed back down, and I immediately changed the subject.

As is widely documented, from as far back as Len and Roy Shaw's first unlicenced Guv'nor grudge match in '77, their ongoing feud (mostly verbal) echoed through the alleyways of gangland London, and continued right up to the day Len was, in his words, *put in that big furnace,* and moved on to his next life.

Lenny had his fingers in all sorts and from time to time he would set up the odd fight for me, too, which was a nice little earner and I always walked away with a few bags of sand. Obviously, Lenny had his usual side bets – he did that a lot, did Len, and earned a nice few bob in the process. You see, when another firm think their top dog will beat yours, then there is always a hefty wager put down on him. The thing is, Lenny and I fought side by side in some frightening tear ups and he knew exactly what I was capable of. The other firm had probably seen their man have a row in a boozer and thought he was some Billy Big Bollocks.

Len used to sort these fights in car parks and places like that. Now, I can't name the pub that I had this particular fight in just in case the gaffa is still active, because I ain't in the habit of getting his collar felt by some aging Old Bill with a cross to bear.

I noticed that Len was already there as I drove up with a mate of mine, so I made my way round to the car park where a circle had been formed and noticed two men about to battle it out. I asked this man what was happening and he said, 'You're late, pal, and they're both arguing about who's going to fight you.' I looked at Lenny, who was properly suited and booted and looked the business. He gave me a nod, and I shouted to these two men, 'Listen, you two, I'll fight you both, one at a time. You decide between you who goes first but I want double the dough.'

So, it's all set, and the smallest of the two steps up first. Honestly, I would rather have had the bigger lump first to get him out of the way, but a fight's a fight and I was ready for whoever. A few men started shouting, 'Go on, Bob, do him,' as he's come steaming straight towards me. I didn't even have time to put my knuckle pads on and he's caught me straight in the chest with some power. It's winded me a bit, but I kept my cool and smashed him straight into his jaw, and he's gone down like a ton of bricks. Well, I'm thinking to myself, that's one of them out of the way, and I'm halfway to a nice bit of cash. By this time, the crowd are all hyped-up and cheering as Lenny shouts, 'Ding ding, round two, fellas.'

The big lump went straight into a bit of a boxing stance and I thought, OK, this could get a bit tricky, so I went into my stance as well, bobbing and weaving, up and down. I feinted a few jabs towards him and, as he makes his way in, I kicked him as hard as I could, right in the knackers. Well, it was an all-in fight, no one said anything about rules, did they? Anyway, he's gone down on his knees and I'm moving around him. As I glanced over, I caught Lenny in the corner of my eye and he's shouting, 'Do him, son, finish him.'

At this point, the big lump's getting up, gritting his teeth in a rage, so I smashed into him with a Tyson combination: one swift hook followed by a mighty uppercut, and it was game over. By now, the adrenaline had kicked in, and I rushed over to stamp on him a bit, even though he was finished. Anyway, a bunch of men grabbed me, shouting, 'He's done, mate, he's done.' The crowd has gone all quiet, you could hear a pin drop, when all of a sudden, this big booming voice hollers, 'Right, boys, pay Uncle Lenny.'

Len walks off to talk business with a man who hands over a wad of notes. Four grand I got paid for that five minutes of work and, if you want to know how much Len got paid, double it and add a monkey.

One night at the Hippodrome, Lenny had popped out on some business and it's gone off big time on the dancefloor. These silly idiots are going at it, fighting, and the horrible bastards are smashing into some local punters who we all knew, and they were good people. At that time, I was working with this well-respected doorman named Richard, who we called Turkish. He was a lovely fella and could certainly have a row when it was needed. As soon as the fight broke out, Turkish steamed straight in alongside me. Just as I ran in, I could see one of these mugs getting all revved up to take my head off with a punch, but as you all know, my job is to stop fights and then just throw the troublemakers out. However, it's game on now, and I've smashed into these fellas and bashed them up proper. I will be honest I had gone into a bit of a rage with this lot because they had hurt a few innocent bystanders.

After the ruck, it appeared that one of these jokers was looking a little worse for wear, so Turkish brought him into the office and was trying his best to wake this fella up, but he was having a bit of a hard time of it, so while he was attending to him, he told me to go and change into some different clobber – get myself out of there before the Old Bill arrived.

A little later, Lenny got back to the club. Immediately, he heard about the commotion and slipped into the office to watch the CCTV footage. Next thing you know, one of the other bouncers come looking for me, saying, 'John, mate, Lenny wants to see you in the office.'

I made my way over, happy as Larry, thinking I'm going to get a bit of a bonus off Len for sorting these mugs out. I opened the door to see Lenny sat there with a cuppa in his hand, and he says, 'John, son, how much rope did you give them fellas?'

'You what, Len?' I asked.

Len says, 'Fuck me, boy, couldn't you have given them a little bit more rope?'

So I replied, 'How much rope would you have given them silly idiots?'

With that, he started laughing and said, 'Well, not a lot, but fuck me, John, I think you may have gone a bit over the top, me old son.'

I went on to explain myself to him a bit, and I happened to mention that one of the lowlifes had had the cheek to call me a waiter. I said, 'A bloody waiter, Len! I'm twenty-two stone with a twenty-three-inch neck, do I look like a bloody waiter or what?'

'Yes, son, you do. A waiter with the hump, now chill out and take a little break.'

The following day Lenny rang me, saying, 'John, the Old Bill are on their way down because of last night. I'll stick you on a bit of a pension for a week or two, boy.'

I wasn't too happy about it because I was only doing my job, after all. Nevertheless, every cloud has a silver lining because now I'm having a few weeks off with pay, so it was a bit of a result for me in the end. Lenny also said, 'Oh, one last thing, John, my mate's just got a new bar in Fuerteventura, and he's looking for a waiter, if you're interested?' Before the phone went dead, I could hear him laughing his head off like some psychopath.

You see, Lenny was a businessman and a professional, not your average thug, so he wanted things done right. This one night, I was working in a club and the owner's son was winding me right up, undermining me at the front door. When it came to the end of the night, my mate's missus was counting the night's takings and I was stood around, making sure there's no trouble, and I could hear this kid carrying on, saying, 'Is he a bit slow?' while nodding his head in my direction.

With that, I've unloaded him, smashing him over the counter, landing on my mate's girlfriend. This idiot was spitting blood and teeth everywhere, so I had it away before the Old Bill turned up.

Next thing you know his dad, the owner, is on the warpath with all kinds of threats about how he wants me sorted and all that sort of nonsense. I was then told that Lenny wanted to see me. He says, 'Come with me into the office, son. I need to find out what's been going on.'

You see, Lenny was on the payroll there, and those that are now upset could have an effect on his business dealings. Len says, 'Right, John, tell me what happened.' So, I'm telling Lenny what had gone on, and all the while Len's laughing to himself as he's picturing the whole scene.

'Right, I'm going to have a walk around there and sort this out. No fucker's taking the piss out of my boys!'

To be honest, it was a bit of a mess. I think the bill for the repairs to his teeth ended up costing him a few grand but thankfully, as it turned out and was always the case back then, they didn't want to lose Lenny's name and reputation at the venue, so it was all sorted and we were quickly back to business as usual.

One thing Lenny hated more than anything was someone giving it the big one; talking shit and sticking their chests out like certain, juiced-up bodybuilders did. Well, you've seen what happened when someone tried to make a mug out of me, but just imagine if they tried that on with Len. One night, this idiot walked up to the club with all the bravado and, without warning, stupidly turned to Lenny and said, 'Alright, Pops?'

Lenny looked at him with a frightening look on his face – his eyes were almost popping out of his head. When the bloke walked off, Lenny immediately turned to me and said, 'Who's that idiot calling me Pops?' I did my best to make light of it, but a little while later, this fella came past the club again and said exactly the same thing. This time, Len responded by saying, 'I'm OK, son!' before grabbing him by the bollocks, and as the man screamed at the top of his lungs, Len said, '"Pop" into my office, boy, and we'll have a nice cup of tea and a chat.'

Next thing you know, Lenny's put his pad on his fist and smashed the hell out of him, screaming repeatedly, 'Now call me Pops.' That leary comment must have eaten away at Lenny for hours. He had taken it as a diabolical insult. It was a liberty too because it seemed like the mug was implying that Lenny was over the hill, an old man. Anyway, I don't think soppy bol-locks would ever use the word 'Pops' near Len again.

Aside from his wild streak, as I mentioned before Lenny was a clown most of the time and would always make a joke, no matter what the situation. Just like this one night when a man and woman had been misbehaving in the club, but instead of resorting to violence, Len took them into the office and had the pair of them writing lines out: *I must not upset Big Lenny*!

So, it wasn't always stress for Len. I mean, some nights down the Hippodrome and other places he wouldn't come into work until about eleven o'clock and, even then, he'd only do about an hour before he would get off home. This privilege came down to his name and reputation – some-thing that he had earned through toil and sweat – and it was that rep that stopped many people playing up in any one of the clubs he minded. Mind you, the other side of that was all the wannabe idiots who reckoned they were his mate or a family member and would try to gain free entry just by throw-ing up his name.

I also got that a lot during the nineties when people had started to learn who I was. This one fella that we threw out of a club said to me, on his retreat, 'I'm off to get some right tasty fucker to come down and sort you lot out!'

So I said, 'OK, son, who is it? Go and bring him.'

He hollered back, 'Yeah, I fucking will! You ever heard of The Neck?'

Well, my pal and I were in fits of laughter as I shouted back to him, ''Ere, son, please don't bring him down – I've heard he's a raving lunatic!'

On another occasion, this idiot was giving it the big one, saying that he knew Lenny, saying that he's Len's family and all sorts of other rubbish. So, anyway, I said I'd go and ring him and find out. With that, I rushed off inside the club and rang Lenny.

'What's his name, John?'

So I told Len his name and Len very angrily said, 'I don't fucking know him, son. He's a cheeky fucker – give him a dig from me!'

I immediately slipped back outside and marked the guy's card, sending him on his way with his tail between his legs like a naughty schoolboy.

As I'm sure you can imagine a wide variety of celebrities used to visit the Hippodrome. Len had a way with people, so he would only need to click his fingers and they would come over. He was a celebrity himself by that time, you see. It was because of this that, though the Hippodrome was a very lively place, it never really came on top that much. It usually only took a strong stare from Len and that would be the end of it.

I do remember this one night when Lenny nearly came unstuck. He was just stood side on to this enormous rugby player when, out of nowhere, this fella charged full tilt at him, like he was going in for a rugby tackle. He overpowered Len and wrestled him to the floor, then quickly broke free and bolted out of the club with Lenny in hot pursuit. Well, as you know, Lenny certainly was not used to being on the floor and, to be honest, it left him a little deflated. He stood on that door all night, waiting for him to go past – he would've smashed him from here to the Watford Gap if he'd seen him again. You see, Lenny was still at the top of his game and, for that reason, he probably felt like he'd let himself down. However, I convinced him to put it down to experience; it was a one-off that could happen to any of us. Still, it showed me that he wasn't an indestructible force, and well he knew it. We'd be sitting there sometimes in work and Lenny would start talking about people, and he'd say, 'Who's that newcomer, John? Who is he? How good is he, son?'

'He's so-and-so, Lenny, and apparently, he's mustard with his fists!'

Lenny wouldn't let it drop. He'd want to know all the details he could. Len was getting a bit older, you see, but I didn't want him to worry so much about all that cobblers, so I'd say to him, 'Why do you concern yourself with up-and-comers, Len?'

'Who knows, me'son, I guess it's just the way I'm built!' he'd say as he shrugged his shoulders.

And that was the total truth; it was just the way Len was, always having to be on his toes. Always having to be The Guv'nor. When Len was ill, I think he started getting worried about going out alone because, being The Guv'nor, he always had to watch his back.

6
ON THE FIRM WITH THE GUV'NORS

Lenny dipped in and out of the criminal underworld and knew a lot of people from it, and some really powerful people at that. However, he was only ever a third party; settling disputes over money for them, collecting debts with me and Al Crossley. We collected for a whole host of known faces, from Charlie Richardson and Reggie Kray to Bert Rossi and Charlie Kray. We also sorted a lot of problems for other well-known people like Kenny McCarthy (Kenny Mac), and many celebrities too, including Freddie Starr and a well-known New Romantic Chameleon, as well as the odd one for the late manager of a much-loved TV duo, to name just a very modest few.

We were always well equipped for this sort of graft, our fists being the primary tool of choice. But, on occasion, your hands would take a lot of punishment, and it didn't matter how strong they were. So, in order to overcome this, we would make pads for our hands that were fashioned to protect your knuckles. We used to make them from gym mats and tie wraps, bound together with the strongest of gaffa tape – this was before the days of the fingerless mixed martial arts gloves and stuff like that, so we had to come up with our own. I showed Lenny a set that I'd made one day, and I asked him, 'What do you think of these, Len?'

'They're lovely me'son, can I have these ones and you make another set for yourself?' he asked.

'No, Len, these are my ones!'

'Yeah, but they look nicer on my hands, me'son. You've done a top job on 'em,' he pleaded.

All this time I am thinking to myself, sod that, they took me ages to make. However, he looked thrilled while he had them on, and his little-boy-hard-done-by routine had got to me, so I told him he could have them. He used them on numerous occasions, but mainly on the doors to protect his hands in a bad ruck. A few years later, I went on to wearing eighteen-ounce gloves instead. Mind you, I kept them hidden behind the door so that the management couldn't see them.

One night, Lenny came into the club holding a bag, and I had one with me too that was similar. Lenny goes to me, 'What's in your bag, John?'

I replied, laughing, 'Well, what's in yours, Len?'

He sniggered and said, 'Well, you show me what's in your one first, me'son.'

So I showed him these brand spanking new, shiny, red boxing gloves I had bought. Len then pulled out of his bag a pair of brown lace-up ones that looked like they were from the 1700s, and I said, 'Whose are they, Len, Laurel and Hardy's?'

Len laughed like a lunatic. He still wanted my ones, though, and was hoping I'd give in, he never shut up about 'em for ages. But I wasn't about to give in this time to Lenny 'The Magpie' McLean.

I had gone around to Lenny's one day and, as per usual, his lovely wife Val had made us a quick cuppa before we set off on a bit of business. We didn't discuss what was going down until we were at the location. So, it was only when we pulled up at this car park that Lenny starts explaining to me that the fella we were doing the bit of work for had been having a lot of trouble from a bunch of troublesome gypsies. *Not again,* I thought to myself, because we had been through this just a few months earlier down the Kingsland Road. However, this was the job in hand, and these gypsies were taking a liberty – they had taken over the whole pub, forcing all of the gaffa's trusty regulars to refuse to drink there. Therefore, after Lenny's finished off telling me a joke, he immediately switched it on and said, 'Right, be on top form, John. This could get fucking messy!'

Now, for Len to say something like that, I knew I had to go to work. Len's plan was for me to go in, start a ruck with them, and then just start smashing them, at which point he would steam in behind me. It was an ingenious plan because it meant that these guys' attentions would all be on me, and then Len would come in from behind and flank 'em, catching them unawares. In situations like this, even Len and I would have to have a game plan, simply because they could quite easily be tooled up, and the element of surprise would take the sting out of their tails. Let's face it, basically, I was the bait that was being thrown in for the catch, the only difference is, I ain't getting eaten up by no one.

So, I've livened myself up a bit, got myself proper warmed up for a row, and walked through the door. Now, I've cleared out some rough houses in my time but, let me tell you, this shithole was on another level. There were a few people in there who I could see looked petrified, punters that were just there having a quiet drink, but as I've scanned the whole room, I could see straight away who the scumbags were, because these wronguns had taken over an entire side of the boozer. Two of these big lumps were stood holding court with their sweat-drenched vests on. I could see a large wad of pound notes on the pool table that they were leant up against, and the rest of the cronies were gathered around them, loud as hell.

Calmly, I made my way over to where they're stood and put down some change on the pool table, indicating to them that I want to play a game next. One of these fellas spouts some un-known lingo my way, which I could only just about make out, but then he said something like, 'Do we know you, boy? Are you looking for someone?'

The other one then came right up to my face and said, 'Oi, soppy bollocks, my man just asked you a question.'

So, I replied, 'I just fancy a game, lads, if that's OK with you?'

I walked over to the corner where the spare cues were, picked one of them up and immediately smashed the mouthy one straight across the head with it – next thing I know the cue has snapped and has shot off halfway across the boozer. I immediately flew into the other one, putting a combination of punches into him. He hit the floor but, all of a sudden, another bunch of them were hanging onto me like drowning rats, and I'm throwing them all over the place. I was massively outnumbered, and thinking to myself, 'Where the hell is Batman when you need him? Hurry up, Len. I bet the cheeky git's out there having another roll-up!'

However, the next thing I heard was the cavalry arriving; there was a mighty roar as Lenny came smashing into them like a mad, crazed rhino, and bodies are flying everywhere. One of the 'erberts dived head first over the pool table, and another one's smashed right into the slot machines – *ping* – I think he's won the jackpot, I thought.

This lot are getting a proper spanking, not just little slaps, a proper ironing out with busted heads and jaws, the lot. I've still got hold of one of the rats, and I've rammed him straight into the wall underneath the dartboard, but this dirty fella has rammed his thumb into my eye, and he's trying to pull my bloody eyeball out. So, I quickly grabbed two darts from the dartboard, and I've stuck them in his head; he soon let go of me and fell to the floor with one dart still sticking out of him, and then Lenny's unloaded him as he's just getting to his feet. By this time, a good few of these idiots have run over to the main doors, and there's blood all over the place. So, we dragged the others out while stamping on them to make sure they didn't get back up.

When it's all over, Len turns to me and says, 'Fancy a nice lemonade, me'son?' before laughing to himself in that psychotic way that was so typical of Lenny McLean. He went over to the lady behind the bar and said, ''Ere, sweetheart, tell your guvnor to get me on the blower later.' Then he turned to me and said, 'Right, shape up, son, just in case these no-good fuckers have woken up and they're waiting outside for round two.'

Thankfully, when we got outside, there wasn't a soul about. We headed across the street and got in the motor, Len turned the engine over, and we quickly got ourselves away from the venue just in case any Old Bill got busy. After driving for a mile or so, Len said to me, ''Ere, listen, me'son, I ain't taking you on these jobs anymore.'

With a puzzled look on my face, I said, 'Why's that then, Len?'

To which he replied, laughing, 'Well, first off, you went in that boozer and had a nice game of pool while I'm outside waiting. The next thing I know you think yer on *Bullseye* with that Jim Bowen! John, that poor bloke had a fucking dart sticking out the side of his head. Look, I've told you before, John, you go at it a bit heavy, not like me – I'm gentle I am, me'son.'

And with that, we just burst into fits of laughter, Len coughing and spluttering because he's choking on the smoke from his roll-up.

Len went and made a phone call, telling the landlord to lose the CCTV footage pretty sharpish. Funnily enough, I had a chat with the fella responsible for doing away with that tape a few years after and I said to him, ''Ere, mate, did you really burn that tape? Because if you didn't then I'd really like to see it!'

To which he replied quite adamantly, 'Look, John, if you and Len tell me to get rid of something, then that's exactly what I do. I ain't in the habit of upsetting you fellas. I mean, I'd like to hang on to my gnashers, thank you very much!'

Anyway, after Len had finished on the blower, he got back in the car and handed me a bit of dough and said, 'Good work, me'son.' Then he reached into his other pocket and started throwing me some more notes.

'What's that for, Len, is it a bonus?'

'Let me give you a little tip. Next time you have a game of pool, always pick up your winnings at the end, alright, me'son?' he replied.

That's when I caught on to what he'd done. He'd only gone and lifted the bit of dough from off the pool table in the pub. It was another excellent result, and an added bonus too for the kids' Christmas fund.

I'd go around Lenny's house a few times a month to discuss debts, and most Fridays, he would be on the phone asking people for money they owed. Lenny had a hard, yet lucrative system. It was like this: for every hundred pounds he would lend you, he would demand an extra thirty back, so that was thirty per cent of the balance. Anyone who missed a payment or was a tenner short would have another thirty notes added on top. This was all well and good when it was going smoothly, however, sometimes even for Lenny it could go a bit wonky. To be quite honest it was giving me a headache, so God knows how he was dealing with it. You see, Lenny had a lot of his own cash out on the street, and I think at one point it was up to a hundred grand.

So, every Friday we'd be at it. You could see him getting stressed on the blower with people when they never answered; he'd be growling at others and if some couldn't pay then a bit more money would simply be added to their bill. Anyway, we're sat there one Friday, and Lenny goes to me, ''Ere, John, don't you fancy putting a bit of dough on the street yourself?'

To which I replied a bit abruptly, 'With the hassle you're having, Len, no chance!'

It was like that right up until the day he passed away. He always had a few bob out on the streets and when he was too ill to collect it, I went out for it on his behalf. I was still collecting debts of Lenny's long after he had passed. It was a bit of extra dough for his Val and her family.

Debts came in from all over the place, and some that we collected, you just would not believe. I was in Lenny's house one day when the phone rang. Val answered it and shouted for Lenny, saying that Reggie Kray was calling. Lenny rolled his eyes at me but took the phone then, a few minutes later, he called me in and said, 'John, Reggie wants a word.'

Well, within no time at all, Reggie was asking me to come with Lenny down the nick on a visit. Lenny didn't go into detail, but I could see Reggie was doing his head in and kept on nagging him about something. Soon after 'as a result of this' Lenny spotted the chance of earning a quick few quid by charging people to go to see Reg with him; people didn't care about it, they would pay any price because, to them, Reg and Ron were folk heroes. Obviously, I had the chance to go with Lenny, but it never came off – I was always far too busy and not interested in that sort of thing.

I was on a night off with my son, James, who I think was about seven at the time, and we were just around the corner from the Hippodrome, so we popped in to see Len. He would always make a big fuss of James, but business was never too far away, even on a social call, and he said to me, 'Don't go planning anything Thursday, John. Got a bit of work.'

So, Thursday came and, unlike any other time, Len actually explained to me that the job was for his mate, H. Turns out Lenny and H had to go to Manchester to deliver some sort of package, which sounds a bit dodgy, I know, but let's just get one thing straight, it wasn't drugs. Listen, I loathe and detest drugs, like I said, and Len was exactly the same. Anyway, the job was to pick up a package and return it as soon as was humanly possible. For this particular bit of work, Lenny wanted me with him as backup. Now, if Lenny McLean needs a bit of muscle, I'm sure you will gather that this was a hefty bit of graft.

The journey was going to be a bit of a drag but, at the end of the day, it was a nice little earner for us both, so it was worth the stress. As we were going to be leaving early-ish the following morning, I got myself up the gym at the crack of dawn to do my training before meeting Lenny at the chosen meeting place, which just so happened to be a right little tasty cafe. Nice one, I thought, 'cos I was bloody starving. As I walked into the cafe, I spotted Lenny behind his usual newspaper, the *Sun*.

'Have whatever you want, John,' Len shouted over. 'Our expenses are all on our boss for this trip.'

A few minutes later, H turned up and we're off and running. However, at nearly every service station we hit on our journey, Lenny wanted to stop for a cuppa, and I remember him looking very uncomfortable by the time we got closer to our destination.

'Find me a carsey, John, quick, I'm bursting.'

So, I drove around a bit lively and found a sign for a shopping centre about two minutes away and thought that would do. By this point, Len had sweat coming down his face.

'There's bound to be one in there, John, let me get out.' Lenny politely demanded.

By this time, H and I were in fits of laughter on account of the speed in which Lenny bolted into the place, with this fast-paced walk, clutching onto himself, mumbling and cursing every step of the way. *Bloody hell, he looked like Freddie Starr when he used to do that sped-up singing bit on the telly.* H and I still laugh about that, even today.

Anyway, even with the endless cups of tea and the copious amounts of toilet stops, we still had time to pop into a cafe around the corner so Len could have another bite to eat just inches from our destination. Half an hour later, we're off for our meet, but as we pull into an industrial estate, Len hollered, 'Don't stop, John, just keep driving.'

Doing exactly as I was told, I drove right down to the end of the road, turned around and parked. By now, Lenny was ranting and mumbling to himself again, and I didn't have a clue what was going on. We sat there quietly for a short while because we had a perfect view right up the street. Then, in the blink of an eye, there were armed Old Bill swarming all over the place. After about twenty minutes or so, from the building where we were supposed to meet, out jumped about twelve police officers with four handcuffed prisoners in tow, so I turned to Lenny and said, 'How the hell did you know what was going to happen, Len? Are you bloody psychic?'

'No, son, they were all in the back of that fucking cafe. H and I clocked 'em when you went to the toilet! That lot left seconds before us!' Lenny stuttered, as he laughed at the top of his lungs.

We left it a while for everything to settle down. 'Right, John, go and see if it's all clear.' I nipped out and had a good look around, all seemed clear, so I knocked on the door of the delivery unit, but there was no answer. The door was unlocked, though, so I went inside where, to my astonishment, there was about six Old Bill searching the place. I held my breath and tiptoed out backwards – very, very quietly – not realising that Lenny and H were on their way in and *bang*! I bumped straight into the pair of them.

'Watch out, lads!' Lenny shouted.

With that, every last one of the Old Bill turned around. Now, I one hundred per cent and without a shadow of doubt know that the package we are holding ain't illegal. At least I think it ain't, but what I do know for sure is that it would undoubtedly need some explaining. Immediately the three of us were searched and asked what we were doing there, who we were going to see, etc. On clocking that this place was a printing firm, I stepped up to the plate and explained to them that we were there to pick up some artwork. They then asked our names; I gave my correct name because at that point we had nothing to hide. Lenny was also in the clear as he had done nothing either. We didn't have to mention anything about the delivery package because, fortunately, Lenny had left that in the car.

After about an hour or so they told us that we were OK to leave. However, we were far from happy because we hadn't managed to get the package delivered, so it was simply a case of 'no pickup, no pay'. Lenny's brainbox was working overtime, so he came up with a plan to wait until all was clear and try to get the job sorted once the Old Bill had gone.

After a couple of hours or so, they all drove off. We sat there patiently for another hour until we saw two fellas creep up to the door and use a crowbar to open it. It was almost dark, but the area was well lit up, so we ran down into the unit behind them. The two men turned on their heels, looked at us and demanded, 'Who the fuck are you?' Even though it was a lot darker inside, I managed to spot that each of them had a gun pointing at us.

'You can put those two bits of metal away for a fucking start, you muggy cunts, or I'll stick them straight up your fucking aris!' Lenny screamed. 'I've fucking had enough of this fucking place, and you two have sent me boss-eyed and won the fucking booby prize!'

Wisely, they moved the guns away from us but still held on to them. They then turned to Lenny and said, 'Listen, listen, are you the London lot we're supposed to be meeting? If you are, then just give us the package with the blanks in – we have the plates with the artwork right here.' Although I hadn't asked any questions on the way down, as was always my way with Len, I had overheard H and Len mention that it was a big pay-off scam to get a big-concern development planning permission passed, and now all of a sudden there are printers, plates and shooters involved.

I started thinking to myself, what the hell have you got yourself into here, Johnny boy? I felt a bit of a panic coming on, but I knew deep down that Lenny and H had every base completely covered. Lenny then said, 'Look, just hurry the fuck up.' And with that, one of the men moved a floor-board, then a wall panel, and behind that was a door. The other one quickly nipped inside and came back out with a package. Lenny went out to the motor and grabbed our parcel. I'm just staring at these two men, trying not to show an ounce of fear because the lunatics are still hanging on to their guns. However, when Len returned, he was hopping about all over the place because he needed the toilet again.

''Ere, lads, is that the bog over there?' he asks, not waiting for a response as he nonchalantly pushes past them with a total disregard for the guns they're carrying. Well anyway, we exchanged parcels and had it away on our toes out of there double lively.

Lenny was quiet as a mouse on the way back to the car, which was very strange for him. We just left, drove down the road a bit and popped into a service station for a little light refreshment.

After our little stop-off, and Lenny's fifth cup of bloody tea, we got in the motor and started on the relaxing journey back. By now, Lenny was completely back to his usual self. He's cracking jokes with H in the car, acting the fool by putting his massive great mitts over my eyes while I'm driving. I'm shouting, 'Len, Len, I can't see a thing!' And he's just rolling about in the back, laughing like a lunatic. We drove for another hour or so, but by that time and all of the day's events, I was getting a bit tired.

''Ere, fellas,' Len said, 'let's pop into the next service station and have a bit of a kip for a few hours, eh?'

So that's exactly what we did. I leaned my seat that far back I was almost laying on H's lap, and Lenny was sprawled out, looking like a big bear trapped inside a car – it probably looked like a right sight to anyone passing. Then the snoring started, and by hell, could Lenny snore. Now, I ain't one to wake a sleeping bear from his slumber, especially one that's the size of Lenny McLean. I mean, it's bad enough interrupting him when he's reading. I ain't on a death wish!

'Prod him, John?' H said.

'You bloody prod him, H'. What do you think I am, a lunatic?' I said back in a breathy, stuttering whisper.

With that, H and I laughed into our chests and left him alone, talking to himself as he slept. He woke up a few hours later, fresh as a daisy, and the cheeky sod sat bolt up and said, 'Fuck me, lads, you pair of noisy cunts can't half snore!'

H and I immediately turned to one another, laughing hysterically.

Well, we made our way back to London and when we arrived, we headed straight over to the bloke's place that had employed us. Lenny went berserk, the bloke didn't know what had hit him; he was almost in tears, the poor fella.

The bloke ripped open the package and said, 'Look, Len, I swear, it contains five hundred invites to my grandson's wedding. I swear to you, this company just did me a cheap deal on the invitations!'

Anyway, that was my job done so I left Lenny and H alone with him so they could sort out the money while I waited in the car. As I sat alone, I started mulling it over in my head, thinking to myself, now I know we ain't travelled all that way just to pick up some poxy invitations, but what exactly had we given them, I still haven't a clue to this day. Mind you, I got a big bonus for my part in that job, so I kept my nose out and never asked a single question, which was always the way with me. If Lenny ever offered up any information, I would have listened, taken it in, and immediately put it to the back of my mind. I tell you what, there's a hell of a lot of forgotten stuff in those dark recesses. Anyway, that little jaunt had taken us over twenty-four-hours to put to bed, but as I said earlier, that hefty little bonus made it all worthwhile, and Lenny and I laughed about it for years.

There was a well-known conman doing the rounds. He must have only weighed about nine stone wet through and was probably only about five foot three as well. Anyway, he'd tried to persuade some big-time money man that he owned a night club and that he needed an investment of about five grand to expand the place. The fact of the matter was this fella only lived in a small bedsit room on the premises, and he actually worked there as a barman, but lucky for him, he could lay his hands on the keys to the door that let you in at the side entrance at a moment's notice.

This one day, when the club was closed, he showed the money man around the premises. On the surface it seemed to be a good investment so, in no time at all, terms were agreed, and papers were signed, and the conman turned up at the office to collect the five bags in cash. The money man said to him, 'One thing I would like to do before I hand over the money is to have a chat with a friend of mine, who says that he knows you.'

The conman immediately smells a rat, reaches over the table and grabs the cash, then swiftly makes a hasty getaway through the door. So, Lenny and I were hired by H's people to get the money back. You see they can't have the Old Bill getting involved, because it's all a bit iffy.

H has had a tip-off that the conman had been seen on the cameras up west, entering the club. Lenny gets a call, and then gets straight on the blower to me and, in no time, we pull up outside and are ready for action. The place has its usual door staff plotted up on the front door, which was a bind for Lenny and me because we desperately needed to see which way the conman fella would leave.

The pair of us takes a little walk around, looking for any sort of cheeky escape route, a hidden door or something along those lines. Lenny, in a hushed whisper that could be heard two blinking miles away, said, 'Look, over here, H, there's a hatch in the wall and a clean patch on the floor!'

'OK, Len, John and I will go in the front and make a bit of a racket, and that way, you can nab the little sod as he comes out through here, yes?' H whispers, in an actual whisper.

But Lenny had other ideas about going in through the hatch. He didn't want to take a risk that he might not come out his way so, instead, I rushed round to the front of the club, shouting the conman's name at the top of my voice. Within about thirty seconds or so I could hear a commotion upstairs. One of the big doormen has caught up with me in the reception area, and he's demanding that I leave. Thinking on my feet, I tell him that a madman had broken in and was attacking people upstairs. As luck would have it, the soppy idiot took the bait and immediately turned and rushed inside to see what was happening. This was handy for me because now I could follow him in, and he would inadvertently show me the way.

As we got to where all the noise was, I was met with an incredible sight, one I will never forget for the rest of my life. There was Lenny with our conman under his arm, swearing and hollering like a man possessed, and Lenny was covered from head to toe in what turned out to be dozens of lipstick stripes and face powder. Lenny had gotten himself through the hatch, but it turned out to be the ladies changing room and it was full of girls who worked as hostesses. When they saw Lenny dropping in through the hatch, they started to attack him.

Lenny was absolutely enraged, he wanted to kill everybody. He smashed the poor bouncer who went for him, and another one who had just opened the door. It was absolute mayhem, and it looked like a bomb had gone off in Danny La Rue's beauty parlour.

'Have you got the money then, Len?' I said.

'No, the little mug must have hidden it!' Lenny grunted.

Just then, I happened to glance over and notice that our little man was a bit fatter than expected, so I pointed to the bulge in his shirt. Lenny ripped off his shirt and there, taped to his belly, was the bit of dough. Lenny carried him downstairs and out onto the street, and I removed the cash from him while he was screaming and shouting as if he was being murdered.

'Keep your noise down, little fella, we don't want the Old Bill making themselves busy now, do we?' I whispered to him through gritted teeth.

Still a little puzzled by the whole affair, I asked him why he had come back to the club. He replied, 'Well, I thought this would be the last place anyone would ever dream of looking!'

But Lenny still wasn't happy and put a shot straight into the conman's temple. Obviously, he dropped like a stone, at which point the three of us left, leaving him in a heap out on the street. In the car, I asked Lenny why he had hit him, even after the money was safely in our hands, and Lenny's reply was a classic, 'I think I heard him call me stupid or something, John!'

'Oh, for pity's sake, he's hearing things now,' H said while laughing. 'Right, come on, I think we'd better get you cleaned up a bit, Len.' So, we were off to the nearest men's shop to buy Lenny a new shirt.

Lenny said, 'You can buy me a shirt, H, it was all your fault!'

'Why is it my fault, Len? Was it not me that told you to wait outside the hatch?'

The attendant of the WC where Lenny went to clean up kept a very watchful eye over us while we were there. H opened up the new shirt, passed it to Len and he managed to squeeze himself into it. It didn't fit one bit, but we had no other choice – it would have to do for the time being. I spotted the attendant fella casting a disapproving eye over Lenny, but I never mentioned it to him because, the mood Lenny was in, he may very well have got a clump.

When we arrived back at the office, the bloke who had lost the money was so filled with gratitude I think he almost wanted to give us all a hug. Maybe because, having witnessed the kind of mood Lenny had been in after being attacked by all of those women, it had made the money man think that Lenny could quite possibly have belted him too. *Result: the job's done, Lenny's a bit happier and we've each picked up a nice few quid.*

By the time we got back to the motor, Lenny was in a jovial mood, so I just could not resist saying, 'I must admit, Len, crimson does really suit you!'

H burst out laughing. Lenny didn't though, he just gave me one of his stares, then saw the funny side of it and burst out laughing as well.

'I'll give you fucking crimson suits you, Len!' he's saying, as the three of us belly laugh our way through the late London traffic.

Another job had come in from H. Apparently, some estate agent had asked for some help when a small block of flats he rented out had been taken over by a bunch of drug dealers – the exact same group of people he had rented another flat out to at the same time, so it was all a bit suspicious.

What they were doing was trading drugs in the doorway of the ground floor, and then charging genuine tenants more rent to live there in order to remain safe, which in my book was a mild kind of protection racket. So, the estate agent had asked H if he could supply a few big lads, since these dealers were also big and very menacing and there was quite a number of them as well. The landlord was terrified by these events and just wanted them gone, so he was willing to pay a hefty sum to whoever just as long as they did a successful job. H contacted Lenny and gave him all the info required. Lenny took it all on board and quickly concluded that we didn't need lots of men, just two or three of us would be adequate.

'Tell the agent we will do it our way,' Lenny said to H. 'It will cost him a fair few bob, but I can guarantee you that they definitely will not come back.' The agent just wanted an end to it, so immediately agreed to the price on the table but insisted he was present on the designated day.

'No fucking way!' said Len. 'It's my way or ya' parked up, son.'

The agent came back to H a week later and agreed to the terms, so it was game on. Lenny calls me up, 'Let's go to work, son.' Just fifteen minutes later the three of us meet up and make our way down to the location.

It's a poxy Monday morning, and the three of us are sitting in the car, listening to the rain hitting the roof, laughing and joking. We've got a pair of binoculars, which I'm guessing H has brought along because they certainly ain't Lenny's – he doesn't strike me as your run-of-the-mill orni-bloody-thologist!

We sat there patiently for at least three hours, just to get a good lay of the land, then nipped off for dinner to relieve the monotony. After talking it over for a couple more hours, we decided to do the job in a couple of days' time, that coming Wednesday, when the nearby local shop was closed for half of the day. That meant that ordinary innocent people might not be about and call up the Old Bill if they saw something they shouldn't.

Wednesday came and, as is my ritual, I was up nice and early. So early, in fact, that Lenny and I even managed to get a training session in down the gym. When we arrived at these flats, Lenny said, 'Let's get this wrapped up a bit lively, lads. I don't want to be fucking about here.'

And with our game plan all set, off we went. Len, H and I walked casually towards the flats. H was in a flanking position on one side of the road, Lenny on the other. I followed up closely, behind Lenny a little. As we got level with the door, Lenny suddenly turned and barged it, and I stayed behind him to watch his back. H waited like a sniper outside, watching the windows, ready to stop anybody who might look like they were going to cause trouble. Once we got inside the flat, we realised that it was only small – it looked bigger from the outside – and what with all the smoke? It was like an opium den in there. All of a sudden, this man jumped up aggressively out of his seat, but he was immediately lifted back over it with a right-hander from Len. At this point, Len and I started smashing anything that moved. Len's kicked the TV off the stand, and he's screaming, 'Right, you no good rats, I want you gone from here, QUICK!'

I imagine that you've seen Len in *Lock, Stock and Two Smoking Barrels*; well, this was the real fucking thing, none of that 'Lights, camera, action' cobblers. The next few minutes were absolute anarchy. I could hear shouting coming from outside, so I yelled over to Len that I thought H was in trouble. Look, don't get me wrong, H was by no means a small fella and could have a tear up with the best of 'em, but by this point, men and women were attacking him from all angles, trying their best to get inside the flat. Also, to that, we could see people from the flat opposite getting involved as they were running out of the front doors onto the street.

A big box was thrown out of a first-floor window, quickly followed by a half-dressed man and a scantily-clad girl. They both ran full pelt up the road, stopping only to pick up the mystery box that they kept dropping, which I'm guessing was full of their drugs and whatever else they were trying to hide from us, not knowing we didn't care about what they were holding. Suddenly, a few big lumps started to run towards the flats and I'm thinking, bloody hell, we're gonna have to go to work here, Len, 'cos we were totally outnumbered.

H was still swinging at anyone nearby to keep them off him, while Lenny and I were wading into them from the other side. It was like battle scene with everyone just running at one another – it was all-out war for a few minutes. Luckily for us, some of these big fellas didn't know their arse from their elbow and didn't know how to land a proper punch. A world away from when Lenny and I hit 'em. They went down like sacks of shit and stayed down.

I smashed into two of them and down they went, but with the second shot, I felt a sharp blow to the back of my head. I immediately turned and could feel a warm liquid running down the back of my neck and I knew straight away that I had been opened up, but I still had all my senses. Listen, I thought, it's going to take a lot more than a bloody rounders bat to put me away, especially with the size of my neck. By this point, the fella with the bat was coming at me again, and I remember thinking to myself, 'John, you have to take that stick from him, son!'

I put my hands up in front of my face and took a bit of a shot across my forearms, but I managed to grab the silly idiot around the legs and rugby tackle him to the floor. There's a bit of role reversal because now I was the one on top. I immediately grabbed the bat and started doing a bit of a Babe Ruth impression with it, and as I'm smashing him, he's screaming like a baby at the top of his voice. Anyway, this fella was all out of fight, so I ran at another one of these mugs that were trying to overpower H and gave him a quick belt too. I put a left hook into this idiot though, 'cos he'd really taken a liberty. I quickly glanced over to see Lenny, who was also unloading shots, and there are bodies all around, pleading and screaming for him to stop. At this point, Len and I caught each other's eye and nodded, as if to say our work here was done. These silly idiots had got the message, and they're collapsed all over the shop, desperately whining while clutching their wounds. Lenny emphasised to them, in no uncertain terms, never to come back or they would get far worse. A few minutes later, from across the street, walked the estate agent, asking H what was going on.

'They're just packing up their stuff, son,' Lenny abruptly replied, and then said to us, 'Come on, fellas, let's keep 'em moving.'

H then said that he was sure he had seen the estate agent hiding over in the bushes opposite. At which point, Lenny jumped in and said, 'How's that, son? Job done, and we personally guarantee they won't be back.'

Just then, as we're walking back into the flat, we could hear a cry coming from the electric meter cupboard. H opened the door and this huge bloke came tumbling out.

'What's this?' asked the estate agent, laughing.

'Oh, bloody hell, I forgot about him,' said Len. 'He was a bit upset about being asked to leave, so I shoved him in the electric cupboard.'

''Ere, ya not claustrophobic, are ya, son?' I joked.

With that, the fella clambered out and staggered out of the main door. The estate agent asked if there was any more, so I pointed towards the basement stairs.

'Well, there are a few more bodies down there.'

'Come on, Len, let's have a gander,' said H.

They found a little heap of them at the bottom of the stairs. Lenny ordered them out of their hiding place and they were begging and pleading for their lives as we dragged them out by their collars.

That was it, the job was finally done, the place was empty, and everyone was happy. But then the estate agent decides to get all cheeky and says to H, right in front of Len and me, 'I'm sorry to bring this up, but I did ask for quite a few more men for this job and there are only three of you, so will that be reflected in the price?'

Well, before I had the chance to open my mouth …

'Listen here, now, son,' said Len, 'don't think for one fucking second that you don't have to pay us the full price that was agreed, because if that's your game, my pal here won't take too kindly to it.'

And as per usual, Len pointed over at me. To be honest, I think the bloke may have been just joking and trying his luck a bit, especially after what he'd just seen as he watched on from behind the safety of that bush.

'Oh no, not at all!' he very quickly reneged.

Well, that was a nice little earner for the three of us, and I must say that he was obviously happy with what we had done that day because we got quite a bit more work through H from that agent over the next few years.

7
A WARRIOR'S ROAD TO CROSS

Right, so far, I've mentioned that I'd learned from the best. In the beginning, my palling-up with Mick Kinane had certainly set the wheels in motion, then a few years later saw me teaming up with The Guv'nor himself, Lenny McLean, as you've just heard, and then last but certainly not least is the man who has been there watching over my shoulder for most of my adult life. This stalwart man, twelve years my senior, who quickly became another father figure to me. You've already heard about some of our capers, but now it's time for him to take centre stage. The man I'm talking about is none other than the fist-fighting, curly-haired, Irish-born strongman, Mr Al Crossley.

As well as what you already know, about him knocking Geoff Capes off his throne to win Britain's Strongest Man in 1984, Al also won both the British light heavy and heavy-weight arm-wrestling championships and, although not massively documented, he had a significant number of unlicenced boxing bouts as well. There was, for example, the widely documented match he had with Dave 'Man Mountain York' at Woodford Town Football Club. Dave had fought and lost in under two minutes to Lenny McLean just a few weeks prior to his fight with Al, but Al put him away in less than half the time – in under thirty seconds. This, of course, was an impressive win for Al, since Dave was certainly not unwilling to stick the boot in or headbutt his opponent if the going was getting tough. I have ultimate respect for Dave and his brother, Roy York, who was a boxing referee, and let me tell you, this man would fight anyone for a few pound notes, and I mean anyone!

Al was a seasoned bouncer, having worked the doors for more years than I can remember, and his reputation preceded him in such a way that he was, and still is, spoken about in volumes around the London pub and club scene. However, for those of you who are a little in the dark about who this man really is, well, I'm going to take you on a trip or two with the 'Viking Warrior' himself.

Al was born in 1952 in Coleraine, Londonderry, Northern Ireland, just a stone's throw from Belfast. My pal, Al, trained in several gyms as a teenager and went on to have many fights, beating all comers before moving to London in the early seventies. Al was a different breed from your everyday man, though, and his usual routine was an early morning swim at 5am, just to start off his day. He would then do some gruelling fitness circuits straight after and finish it all off with the heavy weights in the afternoon, and I mean *heavy* weights.

Al would do his daily regime in Hampstead Heath at a quaint and tranquil little lido. He would pull up outside and dive immediately into the freezing-cold lake. He would then do a few laps, get dressed, jump on his bike, and ride off into the sunrise. I never trained with him at that time because I was competing myself, and the regime I had to take up was a whole lot different; Al was an out-and-out powerlifter, and I remember him once saying, 'You must learn to enjoy the pain to be a true Strongman, Johnny boy!'

I went down to take a look at the circuits he was doing over Hampstead Heath one day, and true to form he stripped off and jumped straight into the ice-cold water. The nearest I ever got was dipping my toe in, and I thought, 'You can forget that! I ain't going in that ice pool.'

Some of this footage was filmed in 1987 and aired as a feature in an episode of the BBC's Bristol series *10x10* on an episode called 'Hardman' that you can now find on You-Tube. Al was like an animal, with power enough to smash bricks with his bare hands. He would balance a block between two butcher's metal weights and hit it full force with the heel of his hand, smashing it into two pieces.

Growing up as a bodybuilder, I was also a big fan of the strongmen competitions, and Al was like some sort of hero to me after winning the British Championships. Most of the events he featured in were filmed for TV, and presenting the 1984 show that he won was the great Henry Cooper. Henry had a lot of time for Al, because Al was a no-nonsense fella, with none of the old cock and bull that you get with a lot of people of his worth.

A little while after his fight with Man Mountain York, I started working the doors with him in Stocks. From our very first meeting, Al and I hit it off, so much so that during nights when I was working elsewhere, I'd go over and see him before work for a chat, and Al did exactly the same with me – we became great friends. I regard Al as family, I'm sure that gives you an idea of just how close we are.

The head doorman at that time had finished in Stocks and Flat-nose Carl went on to take over. Back in those days we didn't really have any solid rules. Al was our senior, and he was far more seasoned, so he just told everyone what to do and when Al said do it, it got done. Now, if there were a problem Al would simply say, 'Look, boys, we only need one guvnor here, and that's me.'

He didn't mean that arrogantly. No, Al's a humble man, and there's no ego-trip there whatsoever. All he meant was, I'll do the managing so that we all know where we are. And it worked.

While minding the door down Stocks one night, I remember Al coming out with this quote, as an inebriated silly idiot asked him for his name and without a second thought came the witty reply, 'Names are for tombstones, sonny boy.' After a momentary silence, this drunken idiot turned on his heel and had it away on his toes. You see, Al knew just when words would pack enough punch over that of using muscle, and that right there, my friends, is one of the attributes that puts Al Crossley head and shoulders above all of the rest. 'Number one – Bosh!' as Lenny McLean would say.

Al and Lenny had worked alongside one another on some heavy engagements before my meeting up with them, and both men had an equal amount of respect for one another. The respect shown to these two men ran parallel in whatever world they moved around in. Al had lightning speed; Lenny always said that he had never seen a man as powerful as Al Crossley which, for me, spoke volumes.

I remember Al telling me a story about the time when he was on some job and an ex-pro boxing world champ had cut him up in his car. The boxer got out, shouting in Al's direction, throwing his fists about, and with that, Al unloaded him; smashing him in the ribcage, quickly following up with a right hook to his jaw, leaving the boxing loudmouth spark out on the floor. If the boxer had been privy to the facts of who Al was, he would maybe have thought twice about challenging him, especially when the road-raging idiot was in the wrong in the first place.

It was different on the door; just a look at the sheer strength of the man would have people shaking in their boots. All he needed to do was tap someone on the shoulder as they walked into the club, just to say hello, and they would nearly hit the floor.

But there were always people who would see a big bloke and, fuelled by the bravado of booze, would want to have a go and this was no different with Al Crossley. There were count-less times while minding the door that geezers would want a row with Al. One particular time, I think it was Phil that tried to warn this fella after I had spoken to him a couple of times.

'Listen, mate, do you know the name, Lenny McLean?' The fella nodded. So Phil said, 'Well, that man you're hollering at is a great friend of Lenny's; they work together. Now, whatever you know of Lenny's reputation, well, that man that you're calling out is of the same stamp.'

Anyway, he wouldn't shut up, so Phil advised him to go into the garden at the back of the pub, in the knowledge that Al had gone in there to have some quiet time. The fool actually went into the garden and about ten minutes later, Phil and I went to see what had happened and this silly idiot was planted upside-down and back-to-front in the gutter, all bashed up. I hope that the fella learned a valuable lesson that night: if one of the boys says, leave it, son … leave it!

However, some people just don't know what's good for them, and a little advice can go a long way. Al once told me a story about a youngster who had done a bit of debt collecting, and soon after wanted to go on a big job with Al. Instead Al set him up for a laugh and said to the youngster, 'Right, sonny boy, go and collect this debt for me. It's only five hundred quid, the guy's only small, and he will pay up straight away.'

Turns out the fella at the address that Al had given was a monster of a man, a well-known nutcase. When the youngster turned up, the man started screaming and growling at him. Suffice to say the debt collector's apprentice had it away on his toes, double lively.

One night while working with Al, it had gone off proper again with a bunch of travellers. Now, the weekend earlier, we had banned a few of this lively bunch from another venue; these were pals of theirs who had not been in before, and there was quite a few of them in the club. They were fighting among themselves but then turned their attentions on us when we tried to stop them. I smashed about five stools over the heads of these silly idiots, so as you can imagine they were dropping like flies.

'For goodness' sake, Johnny boy, where did they all go?' Al shouted.

'They're all down there, Al,' I yelled back as I pointed over to the corner they had moved to. Quickly, I grabbed two stool legs that I had broken off and twizzled them around in my hands like some gunslinger from a Western movie.

''Ere, Johnny boy, you need a bigger holster for those two, son,' Al shouted.

With that, I smashed all the stools to pieces and told him I'd used them all if I had to. Al just used his fists but when it was mayhem in there, I used anything I could find. Al said while laughing, ''Ere, Johnny boy, I've got a new nickname for you.'

'Go on, Al, what is it?'

'Johnny Six Guns!' he chanted at the top of his lungs.

Anyway, we sorted that little lot out good and proper; we did a right number on them. I don't think they came back to one of our clubs ever again.

A few nights later, we were walking to pick up a debt. Al was a few yards in front of Lenny and me because the two of us were talking about something that didn't interest Al one bit. All of a sudden, Lenny turns to me and says, 'John, do me a favour, son, tell Muscles over there to calm down a bit, will you?'

I ran on a bit and tentatively said, 'Al, Lenny said to tell you to stay a bit calm tonight, but 'ere, Al, don't go saying I said it was Lenny who told me to tell you that though, eh?' I felt like a right piggy in the middle and with that, Al turned to Lenny, laughing, and said, 'It's OK, Len, Johnny boy's had a word, I'll stay calm tonight.'

'Oh thanks, Al, that's lovely, mate,' Lenny replied.

I honestly don't think that Len would have ever said anything to Al, just in case he got upset. Lenny turned to me while laughing and said, 'Fucking hell, John, I meant just mention it to Al on the quiet! I didn't mean say that it had come from me.'

Lenny was still fighting a bit on the unlicenced circuit at the time, but he was struggling to get anyone to fight him; I mean, it was quite obvious why no one would go anywhere near him. Then, out of nowhere, Al said, 'Listen, Len, if you haven't got anyone to fight, I'll fight you on a show for a few pounds.'

As I have already mentioned, Al was hard as nails, he feared no man – not even Lenny McLean. Anyway, I said to Al, 'Bloody hell, Al, we're all mates here! We don't want to be fighting one another, do we?'

Lenny must have misheard Al, because he reiterated, 'No one will fight me. I might have to go across the pond and fight in America!'

Again, Al replied, 'Well, what I'm saying is you don't have to, Len. If you want to fight it isn't a big deal, I'll fight you?'

'Nah, don't be silly, Al. Don't start all of that old pony, we're all mates. I ain't having that.'

While this little disjointed chat was being aired in the cafe, I remember thinking to myself, please no, and fortunately, that idea was never spoken of again. When Lenny took a trip over the pond to fight this John McCormack fella, he'd often say, 'It's like when I fought that guy over in America, John. I smashed him sideways. Fucking Mafioso tough-guys – ain't that right, me'son?'

We were all really proud of Len travelling to the Big Apple and still coming back as the underworld's indisputable British champ. He was sharp as a tack, Len. He used to say to me when we were stood on the door, 'Let's hope we have a quiet night tonight, John. We don't get any extra wages in our pay packet for fighting now, do we, son?' Quite honestly, I couldn't agree more with him.

Al had popped round my house for a chat and a cuppa one day. There we were, two supposed hard men, sitting there watching TV. I'm all relaxed with no shoes or socks on, and our little Shih Tzu dog, which I'm sure was possessed, was lying down on the floor near me with his bone about an inch away from my foot. I've lowered my foot down slightly and accidentally touched his bone. Well, with that the thing has gone absolutely nuts and he's trying to bite my toe clean off. I've yelped and jumped back up onto the settee, screaming like a baby. Al, not realising what's happening, has jumped up onto the sofa too – it must have been quite a sight for anyone to see. All of a sudden, Dana has come running in from the kitchen, wondering what all the chaos is, and Al hollers while laughing, 'Dana, look at John's foot!'

Dana looked over to see blood oozing from my toe, and with that, I shouted over to her, 'Get that bloody thing out of here, Dana, it's a raving lunatic!'

I get my big toe all bandaged up, Al is still laughing his head off, and then he says, 'John, do me a favour and pass me my waistcoat.' What I didn't realise was that the devil dog was laid on Al's jacket and he was still bloody growling, so I decided to keep well away.

'You pair are supposed to be the toughest men in Britain,' said Dana, 'and you can't even get your jacket off my little pooch?'

'I'm not touching it!' I shouted. 'That dog's a loose cannon, Dana.'

It was like a scene from Laurel and Hardy; the dog was tucked up on one of Al's sleeves, so he was tapping one end of the sofa, trying to coax it over to his hand so that his coat would be released so that he could grab it with the other hand. All this time, my Dana was leant up against the wall, laughing her head off. It must have looked hilarious. The Mad Irishman vs The Raving Lunatic Shih Tzu.

When all of the mayhem had come to an end, and Al and I had stopped shaking, Al plucked up the courage to walk past the dog to go to the toilet. On his way back he's passed my bedroom, and the cheeky git has said to me as he's laughing, 'Nice room, Johnny boy. So where are you sleeping tonight?'

Al and I were inseparable for quite a few years, doing all kinds of work together. There was another incident with dogs in our story. This one day we were on some debt together and there were two Rottweilers on the drive. I was thinking to myself, *I'm definitely not going in there*. With that, Al says while laughing, 'Here, watch this, Johnny boy,' as he's run onto the drive, growling like a madman at the dogs. I swear, these two dogs ran off whimpering and terrified. One of the neighbours said to me, 'You don't want to go near those Rottweilers, they're vicious!'

'It's not them you want to worry about – it's him,' I said, pointing over at Al walking up the path.

'Don't worry about the dogs, love,' said Al, 'I've sorted the pair of them out. Look, they're nowhere to be seen.'

To be honest, I don't know who was crazier, Al or the raving lunatic Shih Tzu.

Al and I had been called to take a trip up to the West End to sort out a bit of grief that the bouncers there were having with a well-known gangster's family members. The self-professed Yellow Pages of British crime, Dave Courtney, had also been sent down by his guvnor and was standing near us with his heavies. It was quite surreal because Al was taking no notice and reciting a bit of poetry to me, while Dave's face was a picture. Anyway, Dave's patiently waiting and inching his way to us to say hello. When he'd finally got within spitting distance, he mentioned to us that he was just passing, which seemed strange because there had been a bit of bother the previous week that we had been called in to sort out. We then heard that Dave had been sent down to have a word with us. Now, whether he had had a word with the guvnor of the pub that night we do not know, but we got well looked after; each of us being weighed off with a month's wages before we left. Nice result, I thought, but I lost a lot of respect for a big gangland boss that night with the knowledge that he had sent Dave Courtney. Listen, no disrespect to Mr Courtney, but he knows exactly who we are, and what we're capable of. Anyway, after we'd been paid off, Al and I left the place out of respect for our pal, Lenny McLean – you see the gangland boss was a big friend of Lenny's, so it was a no brainer.

It was around this time that they filmed the bouncer documentary in Morden. Al was one of the three main guys they featured. When they asked Al, he told me that he had said, 'I'm working with a top guy called John the Neck, and I'd like him on the DVD with me.'

Unlike other stuff I had filmed where I ended up on the cutting room floor, I actually made the final edit and on to DVD, and you can see me in a scene with Al. Mind you, don't bloody blink because you'll miss me! Al was portrayed on the documentary as a 'softly spoken, self-professed devout Christian'. A man who can quote Shakespeare whenever the mood takes him. But also, a man who prefers handling unruly customers in their most malleable state – knocked unconscious.

Today, my good friend Al lives in a quaint little place and is, indeed, a God-fearing man.

'Johnny boy,' he once said to me, 'there is only one man you will ever need to be accountable to, and that, my boy, is the good Lord himself.'

And the other words he lived by were, 'There will never be a man alive that I would ever be afraid of upsetting more than the man that I pray to.'

Now, if Al says that's how it is, out of ultimate respect for him, I certainly ain't one to oppose it.

8
EARNING MY STRIPES

As I mentioned earlier in my story, I started off working in Stocks with a man that most other doorman nicknamed 'Flat-nose Carl'. Carl was a good man, but he loved winding people up all the time. He would goad in the hope that I would unload a particular troublemaker. Carl's wind-ups knew no bounds. He would even try to shit-stir between me and Lenny McLean. He used to say to Len, ''Ere, Len, that John's a right fucking handful! He can put 'em away easy. His speed and power when he hits someone's second to none.'

To me, this was never done as a friend. I think he wanted Len to believe that he was being challenged in the hope that Lenny would maybe smash me up, but to Carl's dismay, it never actually worked – Len had his number all along.

Carl would organise fights in Stocks. Downstairs, after hours, a group of men would make a circle and two fellas would go at it; I must have had about six fights down there over a short time. One fight had been loosely arranged, and as I was about to enter into the circle, with the crowd baying for blood, the man I'm about to get it on with hits me straight in the face, immediately breaking my nose. My eyes have filled up with water and I can't see a great deal, but unfortunately for this cheeky git, the circle is way too small for him to run away from me. I manage to keep calm, seek him out, and very quickly smash him to pieces. These sorts of pugilistic engagements were soon to become the norm.

Carl had been desperate for me to fight a local London madman called Mad Barry Dalton. The fight never came off, however, but I often used to bring it up, saying to Carl, 'Why did you want me to fight him? You've already fought and beaten him. I have nothing whatsoever to prove!'

If I'm brutally honest, I think that Carl hated this Barry geezer and not meaning to give myself a gee here, knowing what I was capable of, would have loved to see me smash a granny out of this fella. Well, I ain't the type to play silly games like that. Carl still lined other fights up for me, and I smashed every last one of them.

Being a boxer himself, Carl had swift hands and could make a right mess of a man. It's gone off inside the club one time, Carl had a hold of this big lump and he's wrestling with him so I've come in and smashed a left hook into the man and he's immediately spark out on the floor. The whole time, Carl had still been holding onto him as he's going down to the ground, so I said to Carl, 'What are you messing about for, Carl? Just get the job done!' In this job, you see, the quicker you get the job done, the better for everyone involved.

*

On occasion, I would have to fight my way through half of the Chelsea Shed, while the Inter City Firm (ICF) stood blowing victory bubbles across a crowded pub floor. Most of the time I could settle these kinds of aggressive chanting bouts single-handed, but sometimes the threats and taunts would get way out of hand.

Such an evening happened while I was minding a boozer over south-east London called The Frog and Nightgown. It was a lively bloody place, to say the least, and had seen some murderous things over the years, which could have been the reason for its demise as it was subsequently demolished. That bit of turf must have been cursed or something, because years later, in 2007, in the exact same spot under the name of Virgos, the shooting of a woman at the hands of two men took place right outside its doors. I think that it is safe to say that this treacherous little plot of land had seen its fair share of violence and villainy over the years.

Anyway, on previous nights, while minding this particular place, I had noticed that although the other bouncers that worked there talked about having a row in considerable detail, when it actually came to getting their hands dirty, this lot did nothing. I remember thinking to myself, Oh, this is bloody lovely. These silly idiots are gonna be a lot of use if it really goes off! Anyway, this one particular night it did go off and it was a bad old tear up. All hell let loose.

I happened to notice across by this little step that lead up to the dancefloor that there were a bunch of men and women having an argument and, because it looked to be getting a little bit physical, I made my way over to ease things up a bit. I approached it with an air of sensitivity in the vain hope of lightening the mood a little. Now as I have taken the steps up to the risen floor where they were standing, I have just gesticulated to one of the fellas to come and have a quiet chat when, all of a sudden, it all kicks off and the whole lot of them have come flying my way like a tsunami. It's all in my hands now, and I'm just trying to compose myself and get back onto my feet.

The absolute mayhem is spiralling out of control and the lot of them are now on top of me. I've already eyed the instigator of the whole thing but, because I had taken a fall and I'm temporarily out of action, everyone starts kicking the crap out of me. What these idiots couldn't see was me with my hands in my pockets, trying desperately to put my pads on. I'll come back to this lot in a bit, but just for the sake of this story, here's a little more detail.

The likes of Lenny McLean and myself never used knuckle-dusters because we hit way too hard and for that reason, they're likely to break your knuckles. You see, we aimed to put in as many heavy shots as we could; putting more bodies out of the game, ironing out the problem in its entirety, and the pads made this a viable option.

Right, let's get back to the story in hand. All of a sudden, I took one almighty boot to my temple, and it was so powerful a kick that it had dazed me a bit, and everything around me had gone white and hazy. Fortunately, and due to the split-second pause, I'd managed to slip my pads on and immediately I've come up from the floor (afterwards, someone said that it looked like a giant bear coming up from his cave). Anyway, as I've risen to my feet, I started to take slow steps forward and I'm putting shots into anyone that's in front, coming towards me. To be honest, I must have done some excellent work because they're dropping like flies as I'm hitting them, and the crowd has parted like the Red Sea.

At this point, my vision started to clear and I spotted the face of the instigator, the silly idiot that started this ruck off, and he's stood wedged through the main doors so I've made a quick dash to get to him a bit lively. As I've reached him, there's another fella in front of the door so I've wedged him in as well, so he can't move a muscle at all. However, because I had no room to throw my arms around, I'm sticking the nut into him instead and he's fallen in a heap at my feet, freeing up some space. With that, I smashed my hand straight through the pane of 'unbreakable' glass and caught the instigator smack, bang, right on the button. His head went back with some force, and he nutted his pal who was directly behind him in the face, and they've both gone down in a heap on the floor.

My pals from the club across the road have stepped up, and they're helping me out with the lot that had now run into the middle of the road near the railings, and I was fighting with them as they're raining bottles into my head. All of a sudden, someone from the gang ran around the back of me and sticks me, straight in my back, with a seven-inch stiletto blade. I found out later, in the hospital, that it had just missed my lung.

It was so close, in fact, that if it had gone a few centimetres in the other direction, it would have severed my spinal column.

After this lively ruck, I received a phone call from my great pal, Lenny McLean, because literally overnight through the bouncers' grapevine, he had gotten wind of just what had gone on at The Frog and wasn't best pleased. Lenny told me that he had called up the landlord and marked his card.

'That landlord over there will do as he's fucking told!' Lenny told me.

Len's now on the phone to me: 'Right, son, I'm sending Johnny Clark and Andy down to give you a hand, get yourself sorted out, and we'll talk later. Alright, me'son?'

So, that's it sorted. Johnny Clark meets me down The Frog and he's like a bear with a sore head. I'm trying to give him the SP as to who the instigators were and Johnny's going, 'Don't worry about that, John-boy, I'm fucking useless with faces. Listen, when it goes off, we'll smash the whole fucking lot of 'em!'

He was like that, Johnny Clark, no pissing about, no talking. 'Fuck all that shit,' he'd say, 'let's go to work on the cunts.'

Well, that was Johnny's way of dealing with everything, and for the record, let's just say that those fellas saw sense and quietened down a little after our little chat with them.

Two weeks later, I was back minding the door. I really shouldn't have been working, I looked a right mess. I had a smashed hand from the fight and, to add insult to injury, while lifting weights at the gym one of the dumbbells clinked on another one as I was lifting them up and a piece of metal went in my bloody eye. I ended up in the hospital, where they stuck an eye patch on me so I looked like Long John Silver.

It was one thing after another back then. One night, in a rough old boozer, these two guys were playing up and giving the barmaid grief, so I went into the office and borrowed a tape measure, and I went over to them to have a quiet word. Anyway, while my mate's having a chat to them over at the bar, I pulled out this tape measure. I put it on the top of one of the fellas' heads, and I started to measure him. Looking a little bit nervous and puzzled, he turned to me and said, 'What the fuck are you doing?'

So I pulled his head in slowly towards me and whispered in his ear, 'Did you notice that building next door as you came in? Well, it's a funeral parlour, so if you keep giving my barmaid earache, I'll be booking you a suite in there, son.'

I'm almost positive the guy pissed his pants right there on the spot because with that he's said to his mate, 'Come on, we're fucking going.'

My mate looked at me with a puzzled look while laughing, 'cos he never had a clue what I'd said to the guy.

My brother, Mick, was a live wire and always getting himself into some sort of scuffle. I mean, he's no idiot, he can have a row with the best of 'em, but on occasion, he would take on a bit more than he could handle.

I got a call from him one day saying that he's having a bit of grief with some brothers so, as you do for your siblings, I'm on it like a rash. After sorting a few things out, I jumped on the rattler (train) and headed down to my hometown of Hayes in Middlesex.

No sooner had I arrived, and I'm taking the door off its hinges to get to these bullying wronguns. Once I get inside there's mayhem – these fellas are running away from me like chickens from a fox. I managed to put half a shot into one of them, and his legs have gone all funny, and my brother is chasing another one of them out the front door. Anyway, after a bit of a race down the road, a few smacks and a bit of a telling-off, we're on our way back to my parents' house for a cuppa.

The following weekend I was minding this club with a pal of mine called Gary Banks, and Gary starts telling me that it was going off proper next door to him the other night.

'I couldn't fucking sleep for the racket, John. I nearly got dressed and went around to unload the noisy fuckers!'

A little lightbulb went off in my head, and I said, 'Where you living now, Gal?' And he goes, 'I live in Hayes, John, why?' So I said, 'Oh sorry, Gal, mate, that was me next door ironing those fellas out. My brother Mick had had some trouble with the silly idiots!'

Well, Gary and I laughed for a good few weeks about that little story, coming up with scenarios of what might have been, had he come round as well – those brothers would have had three raving lunatics bashing them up.

Talking about good mates, they don't come much better than my pal Andy Jones from Birmingham who, I might add, was another big lump of a doorman. Andy was a tasty fighter and could have a right good old tear up; he was a right lunatic when the mood took him. Andy trained at Dorian Yates's Temple Gym before moving down to London after a little fall out with someone. When Andy arrived in London, I was the first person he met and got friendly with. Obviously, having just got into the city, he had nowhere to go, so we all sorted him out a flat and over the coming weeks and years, Andy and I became the best of friends.

I remember one night Andy, Phil and I smashed up this bunch of gypsies and, in regard to Andy's fighting expertise, I can tell you now I'd seen what I needed to see during this fight. It was clear that he knew how to handle himself and, for that matter, would be useful to have around – a fact of which my pal Andy showed his worth on many occasions after.

We were driving around south London together one day when we came to a couple of big roundabouts. I'm trying to concentrate, while all the time Andy's banging on to me about something and he's putting me off. He then starts trying to tell me how to drive and that I need to be taking the next turning and I'm asking him to be quiet because I know what I'm doing. Anyway, he repeated it but this time a bit more abruptly, so I slammed on the anchors and shouted at him, 'Bloody hell, Andy! I know what I'm doing, mate, stop going on!'

I don't know what was wrong with him, but he took it all out of proportion and thought I was having a right go at him. I carried on driving then all of a sudden realised he had broken down and was saying, 'I'm sorry, John, I'm sorry, mate.'

It is upsetting for me to think about it right now because, you see, Andy had so many issues and unfortunately, there was no way of helping him. He could be a loose cannon at times, which was obviously down to his severe depression. Sometimes, when I was in the car with him driving down the road and someone would beep at him, he wouldn't think twice about ramming them off the road, getting out of the car and smashing them to pieces.

We were working together one night in this rough house in south London when the Old Bill pulled up, lowered their window down, and said, 'Any trouble, lads?'

'Not at the minute, officer, but give it an hour or so … '

I honestly thought the copper would take this as being a bit leary, but he didn't. He just laughed and said, 'I'll tell you what, we'll give you two hours, lads, how's that sound?'

Andy immediately walked in the club and says to me, 'All sorted, John. If that gang of idiots come in again tonight, we'll smash them to pieces. The Old Bill has given us a pair of get-out-of-jail-free cards.

But whatever Andy was running on caught up with him in the end. He was in such a bad way that one day, while walking to his local shops, he just collapsed. I imagine the effects of everything had attacked his nervous system and it simply shut his whole body down. I knew for a long while that he was a ticking time bomb waiting to go off any second. I'd even tried talking to him about it the year before. I picked him up and we went for a coffee, and I said to him, 'Listen, mate, when you're being the Andy we all know, every last one of us loves you to bits. You're the nicest person I know. Please remember that I've said this to you, mate, eh?'

I was gutted when he passed away; he was only thirty-eight and, to be quite truthful, it was hard for me to get my head around it for a long time – silly really because deep down, I knew for years that it was inevitable. I guess you never really think that it's actually going to happen to a pal of yours.

I worked at this top-class venue called Ferdenzie's, previously known as the Candy Bar. The manager didn't talk to me much; however, he did speak to Harry, who was the head doorman there, and Harry used to say to me, 'I think he's scared of you, John!'

'Scared of me? Leave it out, H! I'm lovely, me, soft and dainty!' I used to say.

I had to stop a mate of mine, Big J D, from entering Ferdenzie's one night. You may remember John because he appeared on the front of a book by an ex-wife of Ronnie Kray called *Hard Bastards* at about the same time. Now, Big J D, who was from the US, was massive, and Michael Ferdenzie said to me, 'I don't want him in here!' So obviously, I tried explaining it to him, but he said, *Nobody can stop me coming in, I come here all the time!*

Now, that was an awkward situation for me, but I had to do my job, no matter who it was. Anyway, the big guy got a bit heavy and started telling H that he's going to do this and that to whoever, so I said to Harry, 'Look, if he wants to have a go, Harry, let him in.'

However, Harry said, 'Nah, just leave it, John.' So, I did.

A little time later, however, I spotted the big man on the CCTV monitor. He was outside the club with a big circle of people around him, people that, he'd actually brought along for the show. With that, I made my way over to him – remember, this bloke is colossal, he's at least a full head higher than me – but again, I'm here to do a job, so I went right up to his face and said, 'What's your problem? Look, you're standing here waiting for a fight so just go for it, do what you got to do.'

This approach brought on an immediate change in his attitude, 'cos I guess he could see that I was about to explode, and he said, 'Look, I'm sorry, I made a mistake.'

It was quite apparent to everyone, including me, that he thought his showboating would frighten us. But, like I said to him at the time, it ain't me that doesn't want you in, John, it's my guvnor. Strangely enough, he and I became good friends after that little misunderstanding.

There was a few of us doormen one night. It was quiet, with nothing going on, so this lot were talking football. Now, I'd rather do the bloody washing than watch football, so I turned to my other mate who also hated football and asked him, 'So, what make is your washing machine, Roy?'

'I've got a Zanussi, John,' he answered, laughing.

'Oh yeah? Well, I got a Hotpoint one, Roy,' I joked.

The rest of the doormen with puzzled faces looked over at us, knowing full well that we were taking the piss out of them.

A few seconds later, a fella walked up and said, 'It's quiet in here,' and I replied, 'It's quiet in here because we're here. If we weren't here, it would be a different story, son.' Would you credit it, just a few hours later some idiot kicked off, so I threw the big monster out through the door by his feet. He didn't hang about; he immediately made a quick exit away from the place. The following week he came back and he's calling me this and that, albeit from across the road, so the doorman working with me said, 'I think he likes you, John. He must fancy you.'

Now, I've always been taught to speak or react only if you need to, but then the other doorman said, 'What you going to do about it then, John?'

'Don't worry about what I'm going to do,' I said, 'you'll see what I've done when I've done it. I'll do what I do, and that'll be that!'

My philosophy is, there ain't no point mouthing off in case the man's a good fighter and you don't perform quite as good as you first said you would. This has, and will always, run through my life, and I think a great many others should maybe take heed of that bit of advice too. I mean, they're alright talking about it, but when it comes down to it a lot of these doormen do nothing. Like the time I was working in this one club about five years ago – I would have been about fifty, then. Anyway, this fight broke out, so I've gone flying in, managing to get these two men out on my own. As I've gone back in, I noticed the doorman who had been there a while stood alongside another, younger doorman – this one was 'brand new', as Lenny would say, a bit wet behind the ears. Anyway, the senior one of the two turned to me and said, 'I was just saying to young Mike here, watch John go to work on these two mugs!'

I couldn't believe what I was hearing. Instead of running in to help me, he made the new doorman watch me so he could learn how the top boys do their job. I turned to the silly idiot and said, ''Ere, you're lucky you weren't around back in the old days, you would have been smashed to bits for just watching.'

Even when things got a bit serious on the doors, us lads still tried to have a laugh and a joke about it. Remember, these people I keep referring to when I say we smashed them to pieces were low lives, nothing more; there wasn't a nice one among them. People bandy the word 'bully' around when talking about bouncers but, listen, the last thing we were was bullies; we were simply doing the job that hardly anyone else wanted to do and keeping the real bullies from the door.

One night, this bloke had kicked off and I'd smashed him in the side of the head so fast that I'd put my hand like a gun, blew into the barrel and then holstered it in my pocket. Ten minutes later, I could hear another doorman shouting at the top of his voice, 'Watch out, John!'

This lunatic was only running at me with a big iron table umbrella. Lucky for me I was way too fast for him and managed to dive out of the way and chase him down the street. I must admit, he did catch me on the arm, though, and I remember saying to myself, 'Quicker next time, John!'

There were always idiots about, no matter what place you were working, unless, of course, it was a top-end gentlemen's club because they didn't even try to get into a place like that. What you had to be aware of was staying in control of yourself. One night, in a bar on Borough High Street, this man had been playing up quite a bit, and the other bouncers looked too frightened to do anything, so I've slipped on my training gloves and gone into him. I must have hit him with over a hundred body shots. Every once in a while, I put a light tap onto his chin, just to keep him on his feet. The thing was, I wasn't putting heavy shots into him otherwise he'd have been flat on his back in seconds. I was thinking to myself, 'I kind of like this,' as I stepped my speed up a gear, so it turned into an excellent little training workout.

I went back in, propped myself up at the bar and had a nice cup of tea. Vicky, the manager, looked at me and said, 'John, you need to calm down.'

'I am calm, Vicky,' I replied. I wasn't even out of breath.

'Oh my god, John, I've never seen anything like it! I've never even seen a real boxer doing that sort of thing!' she replied.

'Nah, I'm a big teddy bear, Vicky. That guy just needed a little telling-off.'

Another funny incident was when a row went off downstairs in a club one night. This idiot was on the floor and I was just making sure I did an excellent job on him when, all of a sudden, my pal shouted, 'John, stop!' I immediately stopped, looked up and said, 'WHAT?'

Laughing like a lunatic, he said, ''Ere, John, for a big giant of a man, ain't you got small fucking feet?'

I couldn't stop laughing all night after he'd said that. All evening, I'm winding him up, going, ''Ere, what's bloody wrong with the size of my feet? Like I keep trying to tell you, I'm dainty!'

It went quiet in the club for about half-hour, and then it erupted in the foyer, where all hell had broken loose. This guy comes steaming over to me, and I've put him straight on his arse. I was just about to go into some others when I realised, I didn't have my pads on, so I shouted, 'Oi – Oi – Oi – hold up a second while I get my things on?'

Well, the whole place did erupt then because the other door-men were in hysterics. Funnily enough, it even calmed things down a bit and we were able to get the idiots out of there quick as a flash. I'll make sure to use that one again, I thought.

I racked up quite a few funny stories over at Stocks, with more than one relating to me and my food! You know by now about my on season (in training) food regime. Now, to the on-looker, during the days when I need to carb up, it may look like all I do is eat because during such periods I carry my bags around with me with all the essentials I require throughout the day and on through to the evening. I suppose it might look like I'm some sort of gannet but I can assure you I ain't, it just so happens that I need this amount of food to give my body the nutrition it requires on carbing-up days.

While I was on the door working, it wasn't unusual to see me eating my way through three pounds of chicken. Some-times, at these moments, a row might go off, which was a real inconvenience to me.

'John, mate, those two fuckers at the bottom of the stairs haven't stopped arguing for the last ten minutes. They're going to kick off, please can you go sort it?'

'Oh, for goodness' sake, I'm trying to eat my meal!' I jumped up, annoyed because I'm being disturbed, and headed on down the stairs.

''Ere, fellas, you need to stop arguing, or you'll have to go.'

The two fellas ignore me and carry on as if I'm the Invisible Man. So, I head back up the stairs to carry on with my meal.

'John, they're still at it,' says the manager. 'One of 'em will have to go. You can pick which one!'

Therefore, I ran down the stairs back to where they were. 'Oi, fellas, you ain't listening to me! One of you will have to leave, I'll leave you to decide.'

The pair of them then started arguing about whose going out.

'You'll have to go,' one of them says.

'No, fuck that, you started the row. You can go!'

This went on and on, so I thought, right, you big silly idiots, you're going out! I went over and picked the bigger of the two up in a fireman's lift, then I ran back up the stairs with him as he's punching me in the head and kicking me wherever he can. I charged out past everyone, through the main doors and chucked him straight over the metal fence. He landed in a heap on the pavement and I said to him, 'Right, I said three times that one of you was going. You couldn't decide, so I decided for you, now piss off!'

He never said a word, and when I passed his so-called pal as I was going back in, he bowed his head and wouldn't dare look at me, so I whispered to him, 'It's alright, son, you can have a fireman's lift next time. Have good night, boys!'

The fella didn't hang about, he got off down the road a bit lively.

*

I started to work for one of the biggest door security firms in Britain; this outfit had over 3,000 men on its books, and some off the books too, if you know what I mean. It was a tight business, run by a solid firm of friends. Now, this outfit was like an army – consisting of a vast array of boxers, martial artists, knuckle-fighters and enforcers that ran the clubs, bistros and boozers the length and breadth of London Town. So much so that the guvnors were at one point ordered out of the City under the allegation that they were, for all intents and purposes, terrorists. Now, they knew as well as we did that this was utter bullshit, but it was the only sure-fire way the Metropolitan Police could have them and their 'muscle-for-hire' army ordered out of the City, and unfortunately, there was no opposition intelligent or powerful enough to contest it. The brief was simply that they all had to leave London, albeit a little lighter in the pocket, apparently.

You see, it's a funny old game. The top bloody brass of this leading bank just so happened to drop £400k and all of the firm's banking details deep into the inky waters of the Thames on his way home from work. All of this just hours before their imminent departure from London.

Now, I, along with many of my pals, worked for this firm in many of their large venues up and down London. As luck would have it, I had recently moved into the exact high street where one club was situated. I was called into the office one day, and told, 'John, I want you to go over and supervise the door at a rough house. I'm sure you'll be well pleased with that because it's right on your doorstep.'

'Yeah, that's OK. If it's just up the road from me, that'll do me just fine, mate!'

Anyway, that was that, and I was happy with the new little place I was minding, even if it was a bit of a dive, full of wannabe gangsters.

The reason I was told to go down there was to sort out the lunatics. One guy in particular was a well-known prize-fighter. I ain't going to name the fella, 'cos I don't want to embarrass the man, but what I will say is that he was a bloody nuisance at this time of his life, especially when he was boozed-up.

The manager of the boozer told me that he wanted him out, but he just wouldn't budge. We'll see about that, I thought to myself. Anyway, I went over to the big lump, who by this time had got himself well and truly relaxed, with his feet all over the furniture. I delicately asked him to leave, and he told me to go fuck myself so, knowing this could get a bit heavy, I've smashed a left hook into him, which has taken him down and he's landed about five feet away, asleep on the floor.

I immediately got on the blower and rang my guvnor to report what had just happened. He is saying to me, 'That's fantastic, John,' and instructing me to get back to what I did best, when suddenly I see this idiot again. He must be juiced up or something 'cos he's woken from his slumber and he's running over the roof of the little Bedford van that was parked up outside the place. Still on the blower, I said, 'Bloody hell, this silly idiot is going mental again! Gotta go, I need to sort this 'erbert out!'

I chased him down the road and put a big left hand into the side of his head, only this time he's flown even further and smashed into a lamp post out on the street. He's out cold again, and he ain't getting up too quick from that shot. I made my way over and put another dig in just to make sure he wouldn't be getting up again and all of a sudden, there was about seven or eight Old Bill jumping on me. I didn't put up a fight, I went quietly. They banged me in the meat wagon and locked the door. Out of earshot, and unbeknown to me, the fella came round again and says to the copper that he doesn't want to press any charges – credit to him for that, he's obviously got good morals in that sense – so I'm immediately un-arrested (if that's even a word). I'm on the blower again to the boss, telling him the lay of the land and that all was now well and truly sorted.

'Great work, John,' I was told, 'get yourself back on the door and I'll see you tomorrow to jot it down in the company incident report book.'

That was that. Everything was nice and smooth with no dramas from then on. Well, should I say it was for at least five minutes or so.

It was a great bunch of fellas that worked for the firm. Only the cream of the crop would ever be allowed to work for the company. I mean, this firm got called in for every event that needed security for one reason or another, and back in the mid-eighties, we worked on some big festivals. For one festival, they had anticipated a turnout of around three to four hundred bodies in attendance and, for that reason, the bosses thought that ten bouncers would be ample: three on the stage, three on the main gate and four minding the punters and the perimeters of the venue.

We're all set, me and nine others from the firm, to work the event. A few days before the gaffa's gave us the full SP: dates and times, venue, numbers and event minding protocol, all of the usual arrangements, and we're all set to go – the job is on.

There I was on that Saturday morning, ready for a nice relaxing day. I mean, how difficult could this be? I look after boozers with twice that amount of people week in, week out, but this was my next phone call that morning:

'It's John, mate.'

'Hello, mate, everything OK? Has anybody turned up yet or is it empty?'

'Erm, yeah, it's OK, but I think we may need a few more guys over here.'

'Oh, is that right, mate? Why? Is there a few more than you'd anticipated?' he asked.

'Just a handful, yeah,' I said, facetiously. 'There are about three thousand of the scruffy-looking 'erberts here! To be quite honest, I think the ticker counter at the gate has run out of bloody digits!' I joked.

'Faaaaaacking hell, John! I'm on my way.'

Well, once we got a few bodies down there, it turned into a great event. I looked after the stars on the stage, which was a nice little bonus. A few drinks and a nice bite to eat before we left the event and a great day it was too. The festival scenario was a one-off and was the shaper of many big things to come.

*

The thing about working local to where I'd grown up was that I would often spot faces of people from my past, and not just the bullies like I talked about before, hanging around the Jobcentre. Going back in time a bit, when I was about thirteen, I became good mates with a boy called Pete Dobson. Pete was a year younger than me, and we lived on the same estate. He was a joker, Pete, and he used to wind me up all the time because I was fit and always used to run everywhere. If I remember correctly, I think he used to call me Billy Whizz from the *Beano* comics.

A few years later, I was in a doctor's surgery and, at that time, I was probably unrecognisable because I'd started lifting weights and had got a hell of a lot bigger than I was years before. I was just minding my own business, sat twiddling my thumbs, when I heard a voice calling me, and this voice just happened to be my good mate, Pete Dobson. We had a good old chat and a bit of a trip down memory lane before he asked me what I was doing for a job now, so I explained to him that I was in training and doing a bit of this and that. He then asked me to go for a drink with him, but I had to decline, telling him that I couldn't because I take my training regime extremely seriously, so for a short time that was the end of that.

A few more years passed by, and I'm bigger again and working at the Hippodrome as a bouncer. Anyway, Pete's on a night out with his lady friend, and he spots me working the door; he only just about recognised me, and I remember him saying later that he had to look twice to know it was me. So, Pete walks up to me at the door and gets himself into a boxing stance, saying, ''Ere, do you want a fight?'

Before I had the chance to answer him another doorman jumped on him, thinking it was somebody from a previous row that we had thrown out, and he's just about to give him a telling-off when I jumped in and said, 'What the hell are you doing, you lunatic? This fella is like my brother – he's only joking!'

The doorman immediately apologised and walked off, and I invited Pete and his girl in for a chat. We were catching up on old times, then I said he should come down to see me at work around the corner at Stocks one night; I told him to bring a few pals down and make a night of it.

A few weeks later, they turn up, Pete and his pal. Well, Pete's only been there an hour and it's kicked off, and I've had to get involved in this big row. Crazy too because we hadn't had a scrap of trouble down Stocks for quite a while. Anyway, these two lumps have come flying at me from out of nowhere, and I've uppercut one of them and he's gone straight up in the air, right off the floor. Pete turns to me and says, 'Fucking hell, John, I think you've snapped his neck!' The man was actually unconscious in mid-flight and although I didn't snap his neck, I'm guessing he was being fed through a straw for a long time. I saw him a few weeks later with a head like a balloon. I thought to myself, bloody hell, I knew I'd done an excellent job on him, but I didn't think he'd end up with a head the size of the O2. Oh well, he'll think twice about kicking off next time, I guess.

Another time, there was a DJ brought in for a bit of work at Stocks. I recognised him from school immediately and remembered that his name was Ivan. Funnily enough, he certainly didn't recognise me. Anyway, I've gone up to him and said, 'Alright, pal, you used to go to Townfield school, didn't you?'

'Yeah, I did, mate. Yeah, that's me!' he replied.

''Ere, do you remember a lad called John Houchin from school? What did you think of him?'

To which the bloke replied, 'Yeah, he was OK, we used to be mates.'

'Well, that's bloody handy, 'cos you're looking at him,' I said.

'You what? Fucking hell, it's a good job I didn't say that he was a wrongun then, wasn't it, John?'

That broke the ice, and the pair of us just turned to one another and burst out laughing in acknowledgement of our past together, and I told him about my story with Pete. Pete and I lost touch again but a few years later, in 2005, I received a phone call, saying he and his mate had taken over the lease at a club called Cougar Pinks, over in Great Queen Street. Turns out the previous owner's door team were turning it into a bit of a slum, so Pete gave me a call and said, 'I've booted the old door team out, John. I'd like you to put your own boys in, oversee the operation and tidy the gaff up.'

Turns out Pete got my number from an old mate of ours – top bouncer and well-known hard case. At this point, I wasn't aware that Pete even knew, but I'll tell you about that later. Anyway, I accepted the job from Pete and immediately went in and put everyone in the positions I wanted them in. I took up my post, sat back, and monitored the place with my pal Eddie Jackson (Mad Eddie) as my second-in-command.

Pete's daughters turned up one night when he wasn't on the premises, so I gave him a quick call up, saying, 'Pete, your daughters are in the club, so I'm looking after them!' Pete's laughing down the phone and says, 'John, put them in the VIP section and give them a few bottles of champagne.'

A short while after Pete arrived at the venue. I said, 'They're in safe hands, Pete, don't you worry about that.'

'Cheers, John, you're a top man. Now you can go back to what you were doing.'

'That's OK, Pete. I'll watch this lot and make sure they stay safe,' I insisted. The last thing I needed was something happening to the guvnor's daughters.

When Pete first took over the place, he didn't really know much about running a club and had a bit of a shock when he asked one of the doormen why they had iron doors on the gaff. The doorman replied, 'Didn't you hear about the shoot-up in here, boss?'

Pete very quickly realised the kind of club it was because, on further inspection, he noticed that some of the doormen had bulletproof jackets on. They explained that a little firm from out of south London had plotted up and one of them, who they referred to as their leader, had had a beef with the door staff over the way he was dressed. Anyway, ten minutes later, the place was getting shot at; bullets flying at the main doors like the Wild West. It didn't take a genius to work out that it was those fellas from earlier, but there was certainly no actual proof. The gang had even gone back a few nights later and apparently had a chat with somebody who allowed them back in.

However, I'm in charge now, so I explained to them that we had a dress code and, no matter how much money was thrown about, we would be sticking to the guvnor's rules. A few weeks went by, and this little firm started coming in a bit, getting a bit heavy, running riot like they owned the place. To be honest, it was getting a little challenging to control so I've put a stop to it; I've had a good chat with their leader and it all calmed down. Whether he had done a bit of homework and found out about my reputation is anyone's guess, but everything was nice and calm after that.

Unfortunately, a year later, Pete was lifted and ended up doing a long stretch down the Kermit's. I caught up with him when he was released from prison in 2014 and he's managed to turn his life around. He met a lovely woman, had a new baby and, believe it or not, now works as a probation officer helping people out; making sure that they resist the temptation to reoffend. If I'm brutally honest, I kind of like the sound of that, my mate Pete helping the helpless. See, we ain't all bad.

9
WHAT A GREEDY BANKER

Throughout the years and my many scrapes with the constabulary, it was only on three occasions that I got locked up. One time was an incident in a club, and the second was when they found tools in the boot of my motor; not that I used them, they were just there in case it came on top. But, the third and final time was a little more interesting.

It all began when someone introduced me to a fella while I was minding some club. Now, I'm not going to mention the name of this club because the detail of what you are soon to become savvy is a little delicate. What I can tell you is this ...

The fella that I'm talking about worked for the local council. In fact, he was very high up in his chosen field. Anyway, this fella also liked to have a row and, upon doing an inspection on the club, has asked if he could do the odd night on the door with us. Listen, I ain't some wet-behind-the-ears lunatic, I ain't just going to agree to work with this fella, no, I wanna do a bit of homework first and find out if he's trustworthy. I met him a few times down the local gym that I was using. It seems that this fella, who we will call the Enforcer, also liked to pump a bit of iron at the weekends – he ain't your usual council toff, no! This fella was one of us, well, at least half of him was, if you know what I mean? Right, so, I get to know the Enforcer really well – I mean, he's one of our own. Aside from the fact that during the week he likes to nose around over blueprints and all that sort of caper.

After a month or so, I agreed to him working with us. I knew he could handle himself 'cos I'd seen him on the bags. Also, one day while he was smashing the bag, he'd nipped off to the toilet and when he came back this big fucker had swooped in and nicked his place. Bloody hell, he went absolutely nuts! He's given this fella a dig and sent him halfway across the gym. Moreover, let me tell you this, the big fella stood up, brushed himself down, and left the gym, never to return. By this point, it was evident that the Enforcer can have a tear up. Anyway, Saturday that week he was on the door with me, and an excellent job he had done too.

Over the next year, we became good friends and did everything together. I even introduced him to Lenny and the rest of the fellas. We have built up a good friendship and everything is going along great. One day, while we were having a spot of lunch, he says to me, ''Ere, John, do you still collect debts?'

'Yeah, when the price is right, I do. Why?' I asked.

'Well, John, it's like this. This fella owes this other fella I know a fair few bob from a property deal they did together. But my man has been left short, and I mean proper short, John,' he said.

'What sort of dough are we talking about here?' I asked.

'Hundred and fifty large, John,' he whispered, while covering his mouth with his hand.

'Go on,' I said. 'So, what's the catch?'

'Well, I'm glad you asked that, John, 'cos there is one tiny little fly in the ointment,' he said.

'Right, go on, hit me with the good stuff then,' I said, at which point came the kick in the nuts that I really didn't want to hear.

'Well, the guy we need to get the payment from – he's the *manager* of a leading bank in the City, John.' He went on, 'Look, if you don't want any part of it, I won't say another word on the subject.'

'Nah, don't be too hasty,' I insisted. 'What's my percentage gonna be? Providing I agree to it.'

'Thirty large, John. If you do it, that is.'

As well you can imagine, that was enough for me and I was in. Look, I have mouths to feed! I can't pass that sort of dough up for a few days' work, not a bloody chance. So, with the i's dotted and the t's crossed, it was on. It was a straightforward job, and the relevant wheels were in motion. So, this was the score:

1. His wife works away from Friday to Monday.
2. Bank manager arrives home every Friday at six.
3. We plot up outside his gaff in wait.
4. When he's been back and settled himself in for the evening, we storm in, take him with us, and demand to keep him and do unmentionable things to him unless he coughs up the bit of dough.

5. We know he's good for the cash, 'cos he's taken the lot from the property deal.
6. We take him down the bank for him to get the money out; we leave, drop him off, job done. Hello, sunny Spain!

So, that was the plan. But, did it go according to said plan? Well, let's see.

The idea was for me, my mate Baz and the Enforcer to approach his home, knock a few times and, when he walks up, I charge the door, put him to sleep with a quick left, and carry on from there.

Friday arrives; it's early afternoon and we're plotted up outside his gaff in wait. The toffee-nosed bank manager is already inside, he's been in there for a good hour, so we presume at that point that he's got his feet up watching *Neighbours* with a nice bit of dinner.

As you all know, I'm a bit of a big bloke but at this time I was at my biggest ever. My chest was easily measuring sixty inches, and my neck, well, I'll leave that to your imagination. Now, taking all of that on board, I'm sure it has become quite evident that if I roll up at your door with the hump, you're definitely going to listen to what I have to say. This is the sole reason it was decided that I be the first person he sees. Anyway, we jump out of the motor and head for the door.

I peered through the window as we walked past, and I spotted the manager stretched out on the settee.

''Ere, we're on, boys, no trouble. I'll knock, and when he gets near the door, I'll smash my way in, and we'll take it from there – exactly as planned, yes?' I said.

However, nah, nah, nah, the Enforcer has other ideas. Before I'd had a chance to complain, he's already started knocking. We see the silhouette of the manager coming up the hallway.

'Who is it, please?' he asked from behind the frosted pane of glass.

'Erm, hello, sir, I'm from the council. I'm the local community enforcer officer,' he says. 'We're having a few problems in the area with the local youths antagonising our residents, and, subsequently, there have been several complaints, so we're just doing a bit of door to door to make sure that our residents are OK,' he replies.

'Oh, marvellous, that's very good to hear, officer. Just for my security, do you have a card with your ID on, please?' he enquired politely.

'Oh, yes, of course I have. There you go, sir,' he replied.

With that, he tilts up the letterbox, produces a card, and shows it to the manager.

'Thank you,' he says. 'Just give me a few seconds to take the chain off the door.'

Without a second to waste I grabbed him, bagged him and quickly walked him over to the motor. The Enforcer makes his way over to get in the front seat.

'Oi, he'll have to go in the front, won't he?' I said in a whisper as I'm nodding my head vigorously towards the back door, indicating that I want to be sat behind the banker.

'Yeah, but I get carsick if I travel in the back, John,' he moaned.

'Carsick? Carsick? We're only going three blocks, ya silly idiot. Now jump in the back and quit with the pissing and moaning!'

With that, he gets in the back and we're off. We do what's necessary to put the wind up him, and we're off down the bank to get the bit of dough.

'Right now, be a good boy,' the Enforcer says to the banker.

'You owe what you owe, and you know you have to pay it, it's the right thing to do. And also, if you pay up, these two here won't come back and give you a good hiding.'

'OK, OK, I'll not say a thing. Take me to my bank and I'll make out that I'm on a business meet, and I'll get you the money from the safe,' he said.

'Right, good man!' said the Enforcer. 'You know it makes sense, son!'

I remember thinking to myself, bloody hell, this lunatic thinks he's Del Boy now. He's done more impressions in the last half hour than Mike-bloody-Yarwood!

Minutes later, we arrive at the bank. Baz stays outside ticking the motor over, while the bank manager, the Enforcer and I enter the bank.

Everything is sweet, friendly and calm, as smooth as you like, when all of a sudden, the banker starts squealing like a pig: 'They're trying to rob me, help, help, help!' he's screaming.

I give him a bit of a dig in the kidneys, and he flies across the bank like a missile. Immediately, the Enforcer and I cover our faces and do a runner, sharpish, straight out to the car.

'Put ya fucking foot down, Baz, it's on us!' the Enforcer shouts.

We're off, this bloody motor has never gone so fast! It probably only ever gets a trip down to the church on a Sunday, but now it's doing a trial lap for a championship rally. Once we hit the heavy traffic, Baz slows down and the three of us are momentarily silent. In just six feet of space you can hear a pin drop, the mood is on its arse. I mean, he's seen at least two of our faces, and we're both very easy to remember. Two big bodybuilding types, one with a neck the size of a rhino and the other silly idiot works down the council.

We were done for. The Old Bill was on us like a lap dancer in Soho. They found out who we were, and where we all lived, and then they're banging at my door like a bailiff to nick me.

I'm hiding upstairs behind a wardrobe. Listen, I know the game's up but I'm just playing with them a bit. This copper enters the room, and he's shouting my name, going, 'We know you're in here, Mr Houchin,' and all that other Officer Dibble cobblers. I popped my head out from behind the wardrobe where I'm hiding and shouted, 'Boo!'

It was a picture, as the copper almost shot through the bloody roof! Even in light of what was happening, I just couldn't stop laughing.

Anyway, that's it. I'm nicked. I'm immediately carted off to the local Old Bill shop to await my trial. The court case lasted a full week, and there was no bail granted. That same day I was sent in a sectioned-off wagon to the scrubs for a lovely little holiday. Oh well, I could do with a nice relax. I'll just have to stay in my six by four luxury penthouse suite for the duration of my mini break.

We pull into the yard where I'm immediately ushered from the van into the prison. 'Not what I would have chosen for a few weeks away, but I'll make the best of it, eh, guvnor?' I said to the screw. Funnily enough, he didn't look overly impressed.

We get to the desk and go through the motions. Listen, if you ain't done a bit of porridge (prison time), you'll be a little in the dark as to the regime, so, this is how it went down:

'Right, Houchin, strip off!' said the leary screw. 'Get a pair of pants out of there,' he added, pointing to a laundry basket, 'and grab a shirt from the other one,' as he nods over to an even bigger basket.

Well, I looked like the Hulk by the time I'd gotten this lot on; the shirt was tight as hell at the top, I was bursting out of it, but because of my small waist there was so much bloody material at the bottom, I had a right game with it.

'Just tuck it in your fucking pants, Houchin, you lump!' he said.

I thought to myself, 'ere, that's not very nice, is it? Now listen 'ere, you carry on like that and me and you are gonna be falling out.

As for the old rhythm 'n' blues (shoes) ... well, I've got the biggest steel toe capped boots you've ever seen. I think the full boots themselves are actually made out of steel. I've got this striped shirt on, with most of it tucked in my pants, and the Y-fronts they gave me look like they belong to my great grandad. 'The first fucker to take the piss is having a slap, guaranteed!' Anyway, we walk to the cells and he opens mine up with a massive bundle of keys.

'Right, Houchin, IN!' he demanded.

He then walked away. It ain't bang-up time yet, you see, so the cell doors are all left open. No sooner had I stepped foot inside the cell, and this Geordie voice shouted:

'Oh no, not another cockney fucking wide-boy!'

Well, that was it. I'd had enough by then, and I'd smashed him to pieces all around the cell. Crazy really, because from that day on, he really seemed to respect us cockneys. Oh well, that little escapade came to an end and, after the initial week of being shipped back and forth to court for the hearing, and a month or two banged up while appealing, I finally got off with it – well, sort of.

Something Mick Kinane said to me once I'd got caught will always stick in my mind.

'Right, when you go to court, John, this is what you got to do. You have got to say, "I honestly don't know how I made the statement, Your Honour, because I cannot remember what I had for breakfast."

'The solicitor will then give the statement to the barrister. Then, when you're in the dock, you have to look around the courtroom as if you're bewildered, and when the barrister starts at you with his cross-examining, simply say, "Cornflakes, Your Honour!" As if it's just come back to you. They will ponder on that for a moment and then come to the obvious conclusion that you're a nutter.'

Mick was right, because I followed his instructions and the judge simply said, 'Mr Houchin, you mustn't let people use your size as a deterrent, is that clear?'

Anyway, that was that; I got off without any substantial charges, just a two-year conditional discharge, simply because there wasn't nearly enough evidence. Soon after, my stint on remand came to a finish, and my days as a twentieth-century kidnapper ended abruptly.

I never bumped into my two associates ever again. I don't think the Enforcer fella got his job back at the council though!

10
BROTHERS IN ARMS

I'd had a bunch of operations on my arm, which I'll tell you about later, and I had to have it in plaster for a while, which was a little bit tricky as you'll realise when you've read the next few paragraphs. A good mate of mine called Ian Tate (Taty) called me up and asked if I was available to go down to see a traveller friend of ours called Patrick.

Patrick was a damn good fighter who had fought some top-drawer boxing contenders in his time. I was well up for this and thought it would be nice to have a catch-up with the boys. So, a few days later, we headed up to see our Patrick. When we arrived, I saw Pat with all his family, and they were all suited and booted. Turns out it's a bloody funeral, and what with it being a traveller affair, there were hundreds of people there. A few minutes go by, and Pat made his way over to see us.

'I know your arm's in plaster, John, so here's a baseball bat. If it kicks off, you'll have a head start!'

I said to Pat, 'I didn't realise it was a funeral, Pat. I thought we were going out for a bit of food and a catch-up.' Moment-arily, I caught Taty's eye, and I could see he was thinking exactly the same. Anyway, I said to Pat, 'This is all your family, Pat. Is there a problem, mate?'

And Pat replied, 'Look, sorry, John, there's been a big disagreement. But listen, if it goes off, just stay with us!'

To which I replied, 'Bloody hell, Pat! Of course I'll stay with you lot, there are bloody hundreds of them. I ain't going off on my own anywhere!'

There were some right tasty faces there, and some of them that I have heard through the grapevine are right raving lunatics. As luck would have it, it all went off well with no dramas. I must have looked like a right psycho standing there with one arm in plaster and holding a bloody bat in the other. I could see people looking at me, nervously nodding. Pat said to my mate, 'Fuck me, I only rung you to ask John a few hours ago, and he's straight here. Now that's what I call loyalty.'

Around this time, I was working in a pub where loads of travellers had been playing up, throwing out threats to bring a mob down to do our boys. Well, I ain't having that, I thought, so I called up Patrick.

'Some silly idiot down here is threatening to bring a mob down to do us, Pat.'

'Who is it, John? Put him on the fucking phone!' he said.

Now, I don't know what Pat said to this idiot, but the man didn't stop apologising to me, saying he was really sorry and that he had made a mistake. Anyway, I got back on the phone and he said, 'You can forget about them, now. Trust me, it's all sorted.'

That was the respect he had with the travellers. Pat would always come to the pub and say, 'If there's anything you need, John, just give me a shout.' He was a good guy.

So as you have seen, my life was all about dealing with lorry loads of lunatics, as well as tackling silly little altercations as well, but Lenny McLean and I had another thing in common that you might not expect – our fear of bloody spiders. Yes, that's right, me and The Guv'nor himself, forty bloody stone of fighting lunacy between the two of us, and we're terrified of the furry-legged little bastards. We'd spend many times on the club doors chatting about the size of these hairy gits instead of talking about so-called macho stuff like footy, fighting or page three models of the day.

I was telling Len about the time I'd been training, had my shower, and was just sitting down relaxing and watching a bit of TV. All of a sudden, out of nowhere, came this spider shimmying down its web right in front of my eyes like Tom Cruise in *Mission Impossible*. I swear this furry-faced little arachnid was just dangling there, looking at me.

'Len, I'm serious,' I said, 'I swear the git had a pair of hobnail boots on, and a bloody rucksack on its back!'

Lenny almost keeled over, crying with laughter. I carried on with my 'arachnid from hell' experience, saying that, even though it scared the life out of me, I stepped up to the plate and went to work on the furry git with a flip-flop.

Another time I'd gone in the shower and I was just about to turn on the water when, out of the corner of my eye, I spotted this spider about two inches long inside the cubicle. The thought of this ugly-looking sod touching me, especially on my bare feet, made me nearly fall arse over tit clean out of there! Anyway, as soon as I got my boots on, I became more confident and went back in to look for it. Mind you, I did have my deep-sea diver's outfit on – can't be too careful now, eh?

As I said, my life could go from running from spiders one minute to almost playing fullback for the Dallas Cowboys the next, and this next little jaunt was all down to a good friend of mine, Jefferson King. He starred as Shadow in that show *Gladiators* in the nineties.

Jeff introduced me to a man who wanted me to sign up for the American football team, the Dallas Cowboys. I raised a concern that I had regarding my abilities as a runner which, for the record, was nondescript, certainly for the world of professional athletics. But the man said, 'John, I don't want you to run. Have you seen that man they used to call The Fridge? I want you to be like him, I want you to be a wall, a blocker simply to stop the others.' Therefore, I had a positive think about it, simply because American football was totally different to our sort of football (because, again, I cannot stand that game. As I've stated previously, I'd rather stay at home and do the bloody washing). The American game required more muscle and my strength would definitely be an asset. However, at that particular time, I was training and competing as a bodybuilder, which is a completely different discipline, so it would have had to be one or the other. To be quite honest, when I look back, I probably should have gone because who knows what sort of opportunities may have arisen. Still, there is no point dwelling on what could have been.

Jeff gave it a try but couldn't make the speed times in the position he was needed. He often asked if I fancied joining him over there. We did train together, though, for a long while. Jeff went over to work at the Limelight Club, but things went a little bad for him because he had mentioned to a journalist that he'd taken steroids as part of his training regime, and his name was tarnished for quite a while after. A little later, Jeff was replaced on *Gladiators* by another friend of mine, Mark Smith – better known to the public, I guess, as Rhino. Mark was another top man; he had worked with our team at a club over in Ealing called Broadway Boulevard a few years before.

Mark was a useful fella to have around. Let's face it, if he was handpicked to work at one of our clubs, that's proof enough that he could have a tear up. I remember bumping into Mark years and years later and saying to him, 'Broadway days were pretty lively, Mark. I can't remember myself, but did it ever get too heavy while you were with us?'

To which he replied, 'Well, it never got heavy enough to have to call you over to sort it out, John.' So, I was pleased about that.

Mark has gone on to some huge things. He's moved right up the ladder, living in the US, starring in some top-drawer movies. He has even done a Disney film, and, would you believe it, he only did a voiceover for a rhino character in that fantastic kids' film, *Zootopia*.

*

A pal of mine owned a sunbed shop and I happened to be round there one evening, having a bit of chill out and a chat after having a tanning session, when three big fellas walked through the door. So, I'm nonchalantly leaning against the counter minding my own business, while all the while eavesdropping in on their conversation. I could quite easily see them, because behind the counter it was fitted with floor-to-ceiling mirrors. It was quite clear to see that the two biggest fellas were the other one's minders. Anyway, they started having a go at my pal, accusing him of having an affair with his missus. The next thing you know he's started shouting at everyone in the place, warning them not to get involved. He then turns his attention to me and says, 'Your mate stabbed my mate.'

Granted, this turned out to be true, but this no-good idiot's mate had pulled a knife on my mate, so he stabbed him before he got stabbed himself. Up until this point, I'd kept out of this little row but now this mug had gone too far, and I'd had enough, so I shouted at him, 'Listen, I'll do all three of you if you don't get out of here!'

With that, he's put his hand in his pocket and I have spotted a shooter. I've gone off my nut and I'm growling at him and his minders. Instantly, he gets the wind up and runs out of the door, with his bodyguards in his wake. I rushed outside and spotted them as they jumped in a motor and drove right past me. In situations like this, you just do not have time to think. I mean, I could have backed off and got shot and not be here today telling this story. I turned to my pal, who they had come in to have a row with, and he said, 'For fuck's sake, John, he nearly had his gun out of his coat.'

With that, I turned to him, laughing nervously, and said, 'Yeah, thinking about it, he could have put a bullet in me, couldn't he?'

'You'll get a phone call in a minute, John, because he's friends with someone I know,' he replied.

Well, he was right because a few minutes later the phone rang and this guy starts asking what has happened, so I said to him, 'Yeah, I growled at him a bit, that's all, then he said what he had to say to my pal and then turned on me.' The fella on the phone said, 'Leave it to me, John – it's sorted!'

A few days later, the soppy idiot turned up at the club where I was minding, so I said to him, 'What do you want? You've got no chance coming in here. Oh, and you can take that stupid water pistol with you as well!'

My other pal, Phil, stood alongside me, laughing his blinking head off as I'm giving him the full details of the story, and the Doc Holliday wannabe never said another word, just turned around and left the place.

Around this time, I was on some debt with another mate of mine; we were bobbed down outside the door so that he couldn't see us through the spyhole. There I was, slipping on a ski mask, asking my mate the guy's name, which I have to say was totally unpronounceable. Anyway, I had my mask on, and I'm trying to keep quiet while my mate is trying to mime this guy's name to me – we were laughing that much we almost said let's forget about the debt and piss off home. All of a sudden, this fella appeared. I just stood at the back all quiet while my mate did the talking and then, with that, the talking was over, and we've been paid the money. I will say though that the man's face was a picture when he saw me. Most of the time, scaring people with a look was my job, and in a way, it helped the debtor not to get bashed up. To be honest, it was a similar scenario when I worked the door.

We travelled the length and breadth of the country; distance was never a problem. Because as I have mentioned previously, I've collected debts abroad on many occasions, even as far out as Cyprus. Lenny and I have done many debts all over the UK, including Manchester, and we did loads in Birmingham too. At one time, we were never away from Brummy land; we were up and down the M6 like a yo-yo. People owed money from all walks of life, and sometimes it wasn't just cash we were sent to pick up. On the odd occasion, we could be sent in to retrieve someone's property or even a place of business. Nothing was ever off the cards for us boys. I got that busy at one point that my pal, Big Phil, and I even made Nando's in Putney into our office. We'd be in there almost every day, sometimes twice. We would have our meals in there and everything, and because I was well in with the gaffa of the place, we even ran our faxes through his bloody fax machine.

I went in and out of things with Lenny. Sometimes I wouldn't see him for over a month and then some job would come up, he'd call me for a meet, and we'd be living in each other's pockets again. Just like the time we were working in the Hippodrome and a good mate of mine, Kevin Sumer, popped round to see us. Kev was also known as Kev the Cosh, and I'm sure you can work out why. He was working in a place called Moonlight's, which was just around the back of us; apparently, it had been quiet night at their club, so Kev came round for a chat. He would do this from time to time. As strange as it seems out of all the nights that Kev came round to the Hippodrome, I'm not sure if Lenny had even seen him, let alone been introduced to him, because Len was often out and about doing his club rounds.

Kev was a big bloke and often trained with me on the weights in the gym. He looked every bit the bodybuilder and, in fact, that's where we first met when we were training in a gym over in Chiswick; it was from that meet that we became very close and loyal friends. Kev and I have always had each other's backs, a fact that has been tested on many occasions. One day Lenny called me up, saying that we were short down the Hippodrome and could use another reliable pair of hands. I didn't hesitate and immediately asked Kev if he wanted a bit of extra work.

The night came and Kevin introduced himself to the other bouncers. Then, one of them said to Kev, ''Ere, Kev, make sure you don't stare directly at Lenny when you see him. Just let him see you and come over to get acquainted. Oh, and another thing just to let you know, he fucking hates bodybuilders.'

At that point I could see Kevin had started to twitch a bit, but he certainly wasn't one to back down, even if it did happen to be the formidable Lenny McLean that he was meeting. Kev was old-school, and wouldn't shy away from a tear up, not ever. He would fight any man alive, and that's a fact.

A little while later, Lenny turned up and made his way over to me, saying, 'Alright, me'son, did you sort the bit of cover out?' I informed Len that it was sorted and pointed over towards Kev. Kev, at this point, was leaning up against the bar, minding his own business. Anyway, Lenny walked over to him, leaned on the bar while staring Kev right in the eyes, and said, 'Alright, boy? 'Ere, son, I fucking hate bodybuilders!'

To which Kev cleverly replied, 'Well, it's a good job I ain't a bodybuilder then, isn't it, Lenny?' Kev kept a serious face the whole time and then, after a bit of an intimidating silence, Lenny started laughing. He slapped Kev on the back and said, 'Alright, me'son, you'll do for me.'

Lenny walked off, and Kev said to me, 'Fucking hell, John, when Lenny went all quiet I was thinking to myself – is this the point where he gives me a fucking dig or what?'

I immediately started laughing and said, 'Look, Kev, Len knows your worth because he knows I won't get him no mugs or "brand spanking new" bouncers, as he likes to call them.'

Later that night it had gone off in the Hippodrome, so Kev and I ran in and Kev's jumped on this guy and wrestled him down to the ground, but for some reason, he was hanging on to Kev's legs like a mad-crazed koala bear. I've smashed this other guy, and it was mayhem. Next thing you know the door burst open, almost coming off its hinges, and Lenny comes running through, growling, with two small rounders bats in his hands, and he's piling through bodies, smashing whatever's in front of him.

As Lenny's getting closer, Kev is hitting this bloke, trying his hardest to get him off his legs without hurting him. You see, you had to have your wits about you when Lenny lost his rag. Anyway, we grabbed the lot of 'em and threw them all out, while Lenny's there walking around the room like Rambo, cool as a cucumber.

Anyway, once Lenny got to know Kev properly, he was on the firm with us, and not long after he even got a start doing debts with us as well. One day I was round Lenny's to pick up some details of a real massive debt that Lenny had been asked to collect. We had a nice cup of tea, served up by Val, as usual, and then I went from there to put the plan together. The following day, I picked Kev up, and we drove over to the location of the debt. I'd mapped out the area the previous night, accenting the quickest ways in and out of the place. I had also covered the instant changes that could be made quickly if plans had to be altered.

The job took us out near Windsor, so there was a nice bit of scenery on the way. After a short drive, we pulled up at this massive posh mansion with a great long drive and a gigantic set of electronic gates. As we got to the gates, we noticed that they were locked. What a waste of time, I remember thinking to myself. So, while Kev and I were working out our next move, a man slowly drove down to the gate in his Mercedes convertible; we presumed that he lived there and had seen us from a window or something. This guy, who was a lump himself, shouted over to us, asking if he could be of assistance, and enquiring what we were there for, so I pointed to Kevin and replied, 'Yeah, my friend here wants a chat.'

'Why,' the bloke said, 'who the fuck are you?'

'Look,' said Kev, 'you owe four hundred large (grand) and you got to pay it today.'

'And what happens if I don't pay it?' he asked.

'Well listen, it's like this,' I said. 'If you don't pay, we are going to sort this out!'

From behind the gates, the man said, 'Oh yeah, and who the fuck are you?'

So, in my usual calm and polite manner, I said, 'Well, I'm the man that's going to hit you and *really* hurt you if you don't pay. Is that alright with you?'

The bloke then said to Kev, 'Who the fuck do you think you are, coming to my home?'

To which Kev replied, 'Listen, we want the money, so pay your fucking debt up!'

Next thing you know the bloke has got all leary and threatened to fight us, then all of a sudden Kev jumped in and said, 'Alright, alright, listen. Once I've beaten the fuck out of you, you'll still have to pay the debt up, so why don't you just pay up and save yourself getting bashed up?'

Suddenly, the gates start to open, and the fella walks out. Kev's walked towards him, and I've followed up. The bloke turned to me and asked, again, who I am, and I've gone, 'I'm John!' Next thing you know he's stopped in his tracks and is staring me up and down. I could see that his arse had gone and he said, 'Wait a minute, don't I know you? I've seen you working at the Hippodrome with that McLean fella, haven't I?'

The bloke then turned to Kev again and said, 'Right, so who are you again?' By this point, Kev's had enough so he simply reiterates, 'I'm the bloke who's going to hurt you if you don't fucking pay. And just for the record, now you really are starting to get on my fucking nerves!'

The bloke immediately started to lose his confidence, as his words were laboured, and he said, 'Look, I've told them I'm going to pay.'

Anyway, to cut a long story short, he ended up paying the debt, probably because he had finally clocked who we were. Kev and I made our way back to the office and had a right laugh with Lenny explaining the events of the debt.

11
BOUND FOR THE BIG SCREEN

In the autumn of 1996, a brand spanking new feature film was in the making by an up-and-coming director by the name of Guy Ritchie. Guy had had some independent film making success, but nothing that had put him on the map. His success would later flourish, shooting him and his celebrity profile soaring. With this newfound status, he quickly became an A-lister, mixing with the cream of the crop, so much so that he met, and later married, Madonna.

Lenny had landed himself a part playing Barry the Baptist, and a smaller part had come up for someone to play a bouncer at the casino. I was sat in Lenny's house one day when Lenny said, 'There's a part in this film for you, John. I think it's right up your street, me'son.'

I'd done a bit of TV work in *Hale and Pace* and a few other things, so I knew my way around a script and a set. Anyway, after going for a meal with Lenny and one of the producers, I landed the part.

Now cast your attention back to the scene in *Lock, Stock* where they throw the fella out of the gym; the scene where the big card game is taking place. Well, the big geezer with the shaven head is me. Oh, and just to give you a bit of film fact history, the fella that we threw out of the gym was a featherweight fighter in the seventies called Jimmy Flint. He was an east London boy from Wapping.

I'd been given a script with my lines, and Lenny and I would practise our parts, acting out certain scenes that were coming up. Oh, but wait, all of a sudden there was a change of plan – Guy Ritchie had brought in a professional Irish boxer; none other than super middle Steve Collins, and Steve had been drafted in to play the role of the other doorman. Guy, in his infinite wisdom, decided that he would like Steve to say the lion's share of the dialogue, simply because he was a well-known boxer and he was on the up as a celebrity actor, too. Anyway, I ended up saying one line that was, 'Invitations only'.

Poxy bloody one-liner! Alright, calm down, yeah, yeah, I know – blink and you'll miss me! But, let's get it straight, I wasn't one to argue, simply because it was a job and it was fantastic for my profile. Fortunately for me, I did make the final edit on this one, so I was happy with that. Mind you, if you're reading this, Steve, if you ever have the pleasure of working with me again, next time I'm doing the lines, my friend!

Joking apart, Steve was a real nice fella to talk to. I remember Lenny saying to him, 'My pal here, John, is mustard, he's a number one streetfighter!' You could see that Steve looked a bit wary around me after that, especially with such words coming from a man with street fighting credentials as prolific as Lenny McLean's; a pugilistic lunatic that every man and his dog were afraid of.

During rehearsals, I would wind Guy up, ignoring his direction by doing all of the lines that he had passed over to Steve. Guy would immediately jump up and shout, somewhat hesitantly, 'Hold up, John, Steve's doing those lines now, remember?'

To which I would reply cheekily, 'Bloody hell, Guy, I've learnt them all now!'

To be honest, I don't think he knew how best to answer that. We had some fantastic times on set, mostly because Lenny was a non-stop joker. If you search for the outtakes from *Lock Stock* on YouTube, look for the scene where Lenny is doing his screaming at the scousers bit. Len starts all serious, and then as soon as the scene is over, he starts joking with the two fellas, saying, ''Ere, get me an ice cream while you're at it.' Well, that was Len. Most of the time he was just one big wind-up merchant; he loved it.

Another unknown fact was the door of the boxing gym where the big card game was held was actually the door of a motorbike shop; they had to use that because it was a lot bigger and, as you can see, I was quite a big fella back in 1997. It was a memorable little scene, too. Well, let's face it, it was the scene which the whole film was centred around and, as such, I had gotten it into my mind to make it look as real as possible; it had to look the absolute business. Therefore, while throwing Jimmy Flint out of the card game, I really went to town on it, but Guy thought that I went a bit over the top. He ran in and asked me if I could take it a bit easier on the man, insisting that the camera work and edits would make it look real. It was a good experience being on a film set, watching it all come together. Some days, Len and I would do a bit of training, messing about in the gym on set before filming.

Another good pal of mine called Simon Hayes was the sound man and went on to get an Oscar for his work on *Les Misérables*. Anyway, it was Simon who introduced me to Sting. Now, if I have to explain who Sting is, I guess you've been asleep for fifty years or so. Anyway, Sting was playing the part of JD, who owned the bar that Big Chris's (Vinnie Jones) character was going to move in on for ' … hack you up with a hatchet, Harry Lonsdale'.

Now, I'm not altogether sure if Sting had seen me unloading on the punch bags on set, or if he had seen Len and me having a bit of a spar-up in our makeshift ring. A few days after Simon had introduced me to him as he was coming out of his dressing room, so I nodded over politely and said, 'Sting, mate, you've got a bit of fluff on you.'

Well, his face was an absolute picture: he promptly turned on his heels and fucked off, probably thinking I was fucking about. Anyway, Lenny turned to me and said, 'John, what have you done to Sting? I think you've scared the poor fella half to death!' From that day on, Lenny and I laughed every time it was brought up.

We had obviously been invited down to the film premiere at Marble Arch. I'm sitting there with my pal Al Crossley – Al had been in a few of the scenes himself, you see. So, Al and I are perched there, and the film came to the end credits, and with that, Al says to me, in an annoyed tone, 'What happened to my bits, John?' As it turns out, all of his scenes had been taken out. Well, I couldn't stop laughing, so Al said, 'You're all glory hunters, I'm going to ring that Guy Ritchie up!'

Being a man of his word, he did speak with Guy in regard to this, saying, 'How come you cut me out of film, sonny?'

To which Guy replied, probably while shaking, 'It wasn't you, Al. All the scenes you were in were filmed with this woman and I had to cut her out in the end, she just wasn't right.'

It's a shame he didn't make it into the final film, but we did have a laugh about it on the night of the premiere.

So here I am, it's 1997 and I had a part, albeit a relatively small part, in a potentially blockbusting Brit flick: it's in the bag, and things were really looking up for me. At this particular time, Guy Ritchie was the new kid on the block, with the minutest of backing. However, over a short time, it looked like his name was making its own way in the world of low-budget filmmaking. *Lock, Stock* grossed a massive twenty-eight million pounds from a ludicrous one and half million-pound budget; obviously, my next move was to stay on this Guy's books.

As my acting credentials grew, some bigger and better work came through and I landed a role in the big-budget Nicolas Cage movie *National Treasure: Book of Secrets*. Now, cast your mind back to the big car chase that went through the centre of London. Right, hold that thought for a second. So, I was winding my mate up one day after he had found out that I was in the film. I asked if he remembered the car chase and he started to nod in agreement, so I said, 'Well, you know the scene when it gets to St Pauls Cathedral?' He nods in agreement again as I replied laughing, 'Well, that bit there, they cut it out and that's the bit that I was in!'

My mate just stood there with a puzzled look on his face. Mind you, although my bit ended up on the cutting-room floor, I made it onto the director's cut, so that at least made me happy.

I was also in a film called *Life and Lyrics*, playing a doorman – a lot of that was cut out too, but the doorman scene that I was in made it onto the DVD. Last, but certainly not least, was a film for TV called *Our Boy* that my great friend, Andy Jones, and I got parts in. Now, this little gem was jam-packed with stars. The film was based around a couple losing their eight-year-old son in a hit-and-run accident; it was a very emotional film with great performances from the entire cast. Billy from *EastEnders* was in it, along with Pauline Quirk from *Birds of a Feather*. But, right at the top of the credits was none other than Carling himself, Ray Winstone. Ray was a top man, a proper stand-up geezer, and certainly one of your own. Andy and I were on set for four days' filming. They needed us on set so much because we were in all the scenes that were shot around Ray and his gang.

It was a funny few days, and we had some right laughs. Andy even convinced Ray to do his iconic scenes from the 1979 Alan Clarke film, *Scum*. Ray didn't mind one bit; he was one of the boys. Thankfully, on this film, we actually did make the final edit in a scene inside a church. You can see Andy and me behind Perry Fenwick in one or two shots. Mind you, loads of what we did film over those four days ended up getting cut out for one reason or another. However, you find that in the world of TV and film, it's simply the way it is.

I worked for a few agencies and they got me some good work. I never went to many auditions simply because I knew a lot of people that were involved somewhere along the line, and they would just let me know when something of interest was coming up.

Just as everything was looking good for me, I had an accident which I'll talk about in the next chapter which saw the end of my TV work for a great many years. I ended up having three operations on my arm. It was a terrible time for me because for almost six years I couldn't even train which, as I have said previously, is something I love doing as part of my daily routine. If I'm honest, that accident all but ruined me and, if it wasn't for Dana looking after me, I think I may have sunk deeper down into depression and everything that goes with it.

My arm was never right after that and, due to the injury, nobody would insure me so that put paid to a few things. After a few years struggling, I ended up with iron pins in my elbow, and my right arm was in plaster for just over ten months, but I was determined to get it back somewhere close to what it originally was. Back in 1998, the specialists told me that my arm would never function properly again; well, I ain't having that, I remember thinking to myself, and once I was fit enough to move it about, I started to train in my homemade boxing gym. Every day, I would strap my arm up tight and steadily hit the bag, building it stronger and stronger as each day passed. I still had my Actor's Union card, which allowed me to speak on film sets and TV, meaning that you're more of an actor than just simply an extra. But that was then, and this is now, and I'm hoping to get back filming any day now.

12
THE GUV'NOR'S LAST CALL

First and foremost, I'd like to take you back to my accident and
fill you in on the build-up to it. Right, so everyone has heard
of the film *Friday the 13th* and the old wives' tale of how this
date is unlucky, but I was never one to believe in all that old
cobblers. Anyway, the day started fine when I left on my
journey to pick up Al and Prince for a debt-collecting job – no
black cats were crossing my path, and everything was sweet.
However, by the end of the day everything was about to change
and, because of this, that date will hold a bitter, poignant place
in my heart forever.

Everything had gone fantastic on the debt, and on the way
back home Al, Prince and I decided to pop in and see our
friend Lenny, since we knew that it was the day that he was
getting some important test results back. We pulled up down
Avenue Road in Bexleyheath, where Lenny and Val were living
at the time. Now, Avenue Road is full of heavy, bustling traffic,
and as I got out of the motor, I noticed that Prince had left his

window down, so I quickly ran around to shut it, when suddenly – *bang* – this bloody bus smashed straight into my arm. Immediate, immense pain set in, and I was screaming in agony, holding myself up against the motor with my arm flapping about all over the place. Now, at this point, Al must have thought he was back on *Britain's Strongest Man* when he decided to make a beeline for the bus, but seeing it was long gone, he hurried back to see to me and calm me down in the best way he could. I haven't got a clue who phoned for an ambulance, but one turned up. Everything was a bit of a haze from that moment, but I remember the paramedics jumping out of the ambulance and total chaos ensued.

All around me people were rushing, trying to help. Suddenly, Lenny came running over from his house. Now, I don't know what Lenny was thinking, but he's picked one of the paramedics up bodily in the air to move him out of my way. When Len finally released him from his grasp, the paramedic looked gobsmacked, and stood there in a state of bewilderment.

The paramedics quickly decided that I desperately needed to go to the hospital because I was losing so much blood so, suddenly, we were on our way to Bart's Hospital. Soon after we arrived, they realised that my arm had about had it. It was in a right mess and in dire need of being wired and pinned up to save it. At the time, the doctor said to me, 'Mr Houchin, you're fortunate to be alive, because if the bus had been just half a foot closer, it would probably have killed you.' Well, that was twenty years ago and, believe it or not, I still suffer with it, today.

Now I've said earlier that this date will stick with me forever, but that wasn't down to the accident; arms can be rebuilt, and you get on with life to your best ability. No, that wasn't the bad news at all. The bad news came from Lenny and the results he had received from the hospital concerning his illness. The word that nobody wants to hear: *cancer!*

This bit of news hit everyone as hard as you can imagine. This was the fight he could never win, no matter how hard he tried. Lenny never talked too much about his illness to me, although one day while we were having a cuppa in his house he happened to notice me pondering for a moment at the mere suggestion of it, and said, 'Listen, John, you know it's not curable, don't you, me'son? Look, I know you think everything will change for you once I'm gone, but it won't, boy, believe me, you have nothing at all to worry about.'

'I ain't worried about me, Len,' I replied. 'I just don't want you to go.'

And those few words, right there, were the only ones he and I ever exchanged on the matter. Lenny just got on with it – he was probably in agony a lot of the time, but he would never let on, not for a second.

Even through his illness, Len was forever the practical joker. He told me this one day: he was almost bed-bound, and decided to play a joke on his Val. She had gone to fetch him a cup of tea, but when she came up, Lenny just lay there, pretending he had passed away. Mind you, after Val's reaction, I don't think he ever played that trick again. I think he just wanted to see how she would take it. Knowing Val, though, he probably ended up with the cuppa all over him for that one. You see, that was the strength of the man. Len was that close to death and still fooling around.

Now, not many people were fortunate enough to see the softer side of Lenny. He was like a father figure to me and his wife, Val, a second mother; it's funny really because my own Mum was called Valerie too. Anyway, Lenny always had a way of asking for a drink – he'd shout from the room to Val in the kitchen, 'Val, John wants a coffee,' which really meant that he wanted one. With that, Val would shout back to him, 'Oh, I suppose you don't want one then, Len?'

Val had Lenny's number; she was so used to it by now after almost thirty years spent with him. I think you can safely say, not a soul alive knew Len quite like his Val.

A big day that sticks out in my mind was the day of Lenny's book signing for his soon-to-be *Times* bestseller, *The Guv'nor*. Not that Lenny ever needed any bodyguards in his life, but we were called in just in case some little muggy chancer who might have had a grudge decided to turn up and spoil Lenny's big day. Remember, in our job and lifestyle, we had made a few enemies over the years. I knew how much that book meant to him for the simple fact that he had carried the manuscript around with him in a binder for months leading up to its release. Lenny would often read extracts from it to me, and one day he said to me, 'I'm going to put you in this book, John, me'son!'

'I'm OK, Len,' I said. 'Don't worry about me!'

You see, at that time I was a lot younger and didn't like the idea of looking over my shoulder every five minutes.

Anyway, Wednesday came, and Lenny was due to sign between 1 and 2pm, and the location of the signing was Dillons bookshop on Oxford Street, which today is Waterstones. It looked like the publisher was treating it as a major concern because the shop had arranged a massive display of Len's book, which looked the absolute business; a point of which made Lenny smile, as I guessed it would, especially at such a desperate time.

Lenny was immaculately dressed in a yellow jacket, and he looked every bit The Guv'nor. At that time in his life, he had been known to wear reading glasses but, by this point, with his illness, he was wearing full-on prescription lenses – smart ones, though, Len wouldn't wear any second-rate crap. He had also dropped some weight and was a far cry from the mighty bulk of a man that you would have seen just a little while before, but rest assured, he was still a powerhouse and, honestly, even in his final hours on this earth, he would have leapt into action at any sign of trouble. No illness on the planet would ever have stopped him from doing what he did best.

Len and Val had moved to Bexleyheath over the last couple of years, and that's where my good pal Al Crossley and I picked him up. On our drive up to central London, Len asked if we could pull over for a few minutes; I think the hustle and bustle of traffic in midday London was doing his head in a bit. He was slurring his words a little by now, and it was clear to see how ill he really was, but ever the warrior, he continued to fight on. There was no way Lenny would let all of his fans down; fans that had waited patiently to see him.

Lenny made his way to the book-drenched table with Al and me either side of him. We chose to sit this close because his legs were very weak, and we felt better sitting close by just in case he needed a little support, but to be quite honest, Lenny would rather have died right there on the spot than let anybody see signs of weakness.

Peter Gerrard, Lenny's ghost-writer, sat right next to him, helping him out with the signatures. Lenny looked like the cat that had got the cream, sat there with his books towered up around him. Al and I watched on from our cleverly chosen vantage point as Lenny penned his iconic moniker. Book after book, he scribed without allowing the onlooker to spot any sign of fatigue. You see, this was the strength of the man. He was here on this day, still grafting for the prosperity of his immediate family, and nothing on the planet could ever have hindered him.

A few named faces from the London underworld were there, like Lenny's good mate Johnny Nash. Johnny was a well-respected man in gangland Britain; we used to collect debts for him and his family through Len. The queue was really long and, although he was tiring, Lenny kept smiling and soldiered on, his expression telling all that he had finally made it to where he wanted to be. All the while, deep down, he knew that he didn't have long left on this earth. Lenny still managed to sign every single person's book that had turned up for autographs, and this meant that the signing went on a lot longer than the one hour that was printed on the posters.

Once all of the books had been signed, and the very last person had gone, Al and I grabbed our books for Lenny to sign before leaving Dillons and making our journey back to Len's house. A little while later, and with some careful inspection, we noticed that Lenny had made a mistake while signing Al's copy because he had written the exact same thing twice. Al said to me, 'It's OK, John, don't worry about it.' We both knew that he was tired and had had enough of it by the end of the signing. Anyway, how many people out there have a book that's signed twice by The Guv'nor?

We didn't realise it at the time, but that day would prove to be very poignant in our part in Lenny's final legacy; the very moment we dropped him off that day was to be the last time we were ever going to see him. I spoke to Val in the hope of visiting him, but she very delicately put it to me that she no longer wanted anyone to see him other than his immediate family. Therefore, those very last memories of us all at the book signing will remain forever precious in my mind. For me, that day is written in sand with the tide forever out, etched in my brain, where it will remain untainted. As is life, just thirteen days later, my dear friend Lenny passed away, and never in the flesh would I see him again.

In the blink of an eye, the day of Len's funeral was upon us and, I must admit, most of it was just a blur to me. I suppose it was because I was about to say my final goodbyes to a man who I had looked up to as an inspiration for a great many years. This man among men had taught me so many invaluable lessons and, in what seemed like a split second, he was no longer with us. The tragic end to the Lenny McLean legacy had arrived, and all at the young age of just forty-nine; for me, none of it made any sense.

On the morning of the funeral, me and a few of my close mates, Al, Kev and Big Phil Jennings, met up for a spot of breakfast and a chat, gearing ourselves up for the drive over to Lenny's house in Bexleyheath. A mass of people had gathered, and everyone was shaking each other's hands. I made my way over to Len's son, Jamie, who was stood with the *EastEnders* actor Craig Fairbrass. We said our hellos and shook hands, but none of us had much to say though simply because we were all still in a state of shock.

I was asked by Val if we would like to travel down in the family and friends' car, which of course I found a complete honour. Obviously, the immediate family went in the first car, and Al and I followed on in the second. I'm racking my brain now trying to remember who else was in there with us. I honestly cannot recall; it was all just a haze. My mates Kevin Sumer and Billy Isaac, an ex-professional boxer who looked up to Len like no other, were in another car directly behind us. It felt like the drive went on for hours. The streets were jam-packed with people, which was amazing to see; it proved to be a real heart-warming show of respect for my friend, Len.

As we arrived at the crematorium, I noticed a great many well-known underworld figures were there to pay their respects. Gangland bosses like Charlie Richardson nodded and said hello, among others. There were also the likes of Tony Lambrianou and, alongside him, Lenny's on-and-off driver, Eddie

David. There were so many more faces, but I'd be here all day trying to recollect. I was asked by Val to go inside with her. I obliged, then made my way up to the front. I sat down at the side of Lenny's writer, Peter Gerrard. I said hello, he said hello back, and we comforted one another with a friendly shaking of hands.

After the service, and at Val's request, I went back to their house for a chat and a cup of tea. Now, as fans of Lenny McLean, I am sure you will have seen photographs of the procession with its thousands of well-wishers lining the East End streets that were in the national press. Well, it was a procession and a service fit for a king. Lenny's wife and family had undoubtedly done the man proud. My dear friend Len had been gifted with a fantastic send-off. Mind you, Lenny knew that's the way it would be because he'd insisted on it time after time, as him and Val talked it over.

Most people will not have had the privilege to know the Lenny McLean that the likes of Al Crossley and I had the pleasure to know. Lenny was a comedian, but also very kind and generous. He was a loyal friend and, of course, fearless. Lenny was everything you would imagine – he had hands like King Kong and a voice that sounded like a bucket of nuts and bolts, and when Lenny McLean got the raving hump, well, the only thing I could say on that score is, you better get out of his bloody way!

Lenny said on so many occasions that it was not a life that he chose, it was a life that crept up on him, and I have to agree with him there. Having said that, I wouldn't have had it any other way. Meeting Lenny was the business at that time – everybody wanted to be in and around the great man and I, of course, was no exception. He was a very charismatic and formidable character, to say the least. Yes, of course, he had that other side to him which could sometimes make for a hard day's work, but since Lenny was on offer twenty-four-seven, you had to have your wits about you at all times; in that I mean, you couldn't really have an off day around him. Put it like this, anyone can do a regular nine to five job and take a day off sick, but that simply was not the case with us, because there was always some little firm out there that would want to challenge you. Lenny was always there for me and, in turn, I would like to think that Al and I were there for him too. Standing by him, through the good and the bad, right up until the day he passed away.

Lenny taught me so many of life's lessons, and for that I am incredibly grateful. I still cannot believe it is twenty years since he passed away because, to me, it almost feels like yesterday. I would like to reiterate something Lenny once said on the Richard Littlejohn Show a few months before he died.

'There's ten thousand street-fighters out there who ain't getting a tanner. Well, I'm a one-off – I'm The Guv'nor.'

13
THE SNATCH SQUAD

As we inched steadily towards the year 2000, I was still working with the boys – Al and a few other top doormen, many that I have previously mentioned but, if I haven't, hold yer horses, 'cos you'll all get a mention. At this time in my life, I had ventured into the slightly more civilised world of events and music festivals. I mean, yes, I kept my hand in with the bodyguarding and debt collecting because that was my bread and butter, that's what put food on the table. Anyway, while working on the festivals, we were rewarded with a little naughty nickname. It was direct and straight to the point: we were known as The Snatch Squad.

Our reputation was as an elite and well-oiled crew, patrolling around in a jeep, awaiting instruction from the hierarchy for us to saddle up and sort out trouble – trouble that the regular security boys were ill-equipped to handle. To put it into layman's terms, we were seen as a bunch of tasty, fist-fighting lunatics without a care in the world. If I'm honest, the same could be said for us while working the doors. I'd always worked with good people; people that would have your back in a heartbeat and vice versa. Over the pages of this chapter, I am going to tell you a few stories regarding the many bodies of muscle that were part of our little firm. This staunch and reliable set of fist-fighting men are still my friends to this day.

Mark Robbins was a really good mate of mine. About ten years ago, he was working at a place run by a friend of ours, who you will hear about shortly, called Kiran. Big Kiran took over the door at a club in Mayfair and, when he did, he immediately phoned me up because he wanted me to work alongside them.

Mark was telling me one day how this one old-school doorman couldn't get a licence because he was a raving lunatic and the doorman said to Mark, laughing, 'In that case, Mark, how the fuck has John the Neck got a licence? I can't get one and he's more of a raving lunatic than I've ever been!'

We were working this festival – Mark, Big Kiran and another top man and great friend called Roy. No one messed with Roy either, he was another handy fella. Anyway, it was our first night and starting to get dark. Now, I'm driving, but with it being the first night, I didn't have a clue what was in front of me; suffice to say, I hadn't managed to see the tent that was right in front of my eyes and with that, I drove straight over this poor fella's leg – I've only gone and broken it.

The festivals were relatively calm for the most part, but at night, things would always get a bit silly, simply because people had had too much booze down them and had started getting stupid, doing things like setting fire to tents and even each other. The four of us would be trying to put these fires out, but you'd have pisshead idiots throwing Smirnoff bottles at us, just for a laugh, as we passed by them. This was a bit annoying because there were so many people there, we couldn't prove who had done it.

There would be kids there drugged up off their heads, and you already know how I feel about drugs. What we'd do is try and find out who the dealers were and throw them out, taking their armbands off them to stop them getting back in. The same went for the bullies who were picking fights with kids – they went out the exact same way but with a little more force. We kept all of their armbands and sold them on to other punters for a bit of extra cash.

Another good mate of mine to this day is big Scott Chisolm. I first met Scott in the eighties, and over the years, we met up on specific jobs from time to time. When Scott was working in a place called Browns, he met the actor Charlie Sheen and, in no time at all, was offered a small part in his film, *The Three Musketeers*. From what I remember, Charlie asked him to go to America to bodyguard him and he ended doing that for five years, too. Scott's name very quickly became known in and around Hollywood, and he ended up doing bodyguard work for a great many A-listers; the likes of Michelle Pfeiffer, Robert De Niro, Nicole Kidman to name but a few. Funnily enough, on his return back to the UK, Scott's name had travelled back across the pond and an influx of bodyguard work in the UK came flooding in here for him as well.

He started his own security company with another good mate of ours, Steve Sango, or Sanga as he was known among the boys. I did quite a bit of work for these two's firm, too. I remember working the Reading Festival. We used to do all of the VIP areas, we were in a snatch squad again, and when they had big problems, we would go in heavy and sort the trouble out. To be honest, it was always the same: just the usual pissed-up revellers trying to get in for free by coming over the fence, but one time the radio goes off, and we make our way to the back of the stage, and we see all of the bloody roadies (road crew) having a tear up with each other. Immediately, we jump in to break it up and then these idiots have the cheek to turn on us. Well, so be it, 'cos after a few minutes there are bodies all around the place, and not long after the Old Bill turned up and got involved: Sanga and Big Scotty got lifted and spent the night in Reading police cells; they weren't bloody happy, to say the least.

I went on to do a lot of stuff with Scotty, from cleaning up naughty boozers to collecting debts together. Before long, he moved on and worked on hundreds of top films. Scotty is a well-known and much sought-after bodyguard to some of the biggest stars in the world today.

It's a nice day out, but I'm stuck in the gym – can't break the daily routine, it's just not the way I live my life. Anyway, I'm on the heavy machinery because I'm built like a monster (everyone else's words, not mine!). I'm minding my own business when this little fella makes his way over to me; I'm guessing he's about five foot eight, tops. Later that day I found out that his name was Mick (Mickey to his pals) and he's a goalkeeper, which wasn't of that much interest to me since I don't like foot-ball, but he's also a drummer, so I'm a bit more interested because I've bashed about a bit on the skins myself here and there. Anyway, back to our first meet. So, this Mickey fella comes strolling over to me, cool as you like, rolling his sleeves up on the way over. 'You see this?' he says, pointing to his arms, which were like Mr Puniverse next to mine. 'Well, that's what you should be aiming for, son!'

I couldn't believe my ears – I didn't know where to look and, to be honest, I almost burst out laughing. From that moment on, this Mickey fella and I hit it right off and became fantastic friends. Soon after, Mickey lost his job and the fellas and I looked after him, we sort of took him under our wing. He went everywhere with us; we even took him to work at old Wembley, where we headed up the security. Back in those days, long before all of the red tape, working at Wembley was a great little number. You see, we were mobile. Not just stood on the gates like the others, no: we would mooch around the place looking for wrongguns that were selling counterfeit stuff inside the perimeter. Some-times, when we were parked up somewhere having a coffee, we would wait to get a call and then we'd liven ourselves up and go and sort whatever problem was reported to us. Our little firm usually consisted of about twelve of us and the other security teams would refer to us as the 'heavy mob'. Now, that's not nice, is it? We were a friendly bunch of fel-las! Joking apart, wherever our firm was sent, the trouble automatically calmed down.

For those of you that ain't been to old Wembley Stadium, Olympic Way led right from the train station up to the grounds, so we were doing our patrol up there. It was busy enough, but most of the punters were inside ready for the event. I don't remember who but one of our firms spotted this big ginger bloke, he was absolutely massive. Anyway, he was with a smaller man, and they're on the make down the way, selling counterfeit glow-in-the-dark items. With that, one of my boys – Big Phil Jennings aka The Honey Monster – goes over to this man to take the stuff from him, but the fella starts giving the big one saying, 'Right, come on, we'll have a fucking straightener, then.' So, Mickey, who was at least half of his size, jumps in and says, 'Listen, you don't want to be having a straightener with him, I'm telling ya!'

However, soppy bollocks just kept on giving it large so I stepped in and said, 'Listen, now, we don't know who you are, and you don't know who we are, so why don't you keep quiet and let's not turn this into something neither of us wants?' At this point, a copper came over and tried to calm it down. The big ginger idiot comes over to us and starts apologising. I guess his bottle had gone, and he was trying to make amends – either that or the Old Bill had told him exactly who we were; everyone knew what we were capable of.

It was an excellent little number working there. We used to pop into this kebab shop and get a bit of lunch, then we would just hang about on the corner, sunbathing and cracking jokes with everyone as they went by – and remember, we were getting paid for this. The boss would mooch past from time to time and say, 'Alright, fellas, have you got it all covered?'

Every time I'd reply, 'Yeah, all good, mate, we're just off over the other side for a look.' Then we would go off and have an ice cream or something. Now, don't get me wrong, when it went off and they radioed us we'd be there at the drop of a hat, sometimes with our ice creams still dripping down our hands. I remember one night while doing a shift my car got clamped. Now, I could have lost the plot right there and then, but instead I went over and spoke nicely to the man, real polite, and it worked because the next thing you know this fella has unclamped it. You see, violence is not always the solution – in this instance, I used emotion over aggression and it worked, or maybe he'd seen the size of our team and thought better of it.

Round this time, I moved to a new house and built a big, all-purpose gym in my garage. I had the lot in there, it was absolute mustard. Mickey always came over and he and I would do a few rounds on the bags, then we'd swap and I would take him on the bag and show him how to use his weight to hit properly. I didn't half cause a stink one day because I put these great big iron doors on to stop us getting robbed, but the next thing you know, I'm being grassed up to the council by some lowlife rat for having my gym in there.

I once got a call from Mick saying that his missus was on her way home from work and these men had given her a load of shit outside this pub as she was passing by in her car.

'It's really upset her, John! About ten of these men came out of the pub and spat all over her car window, and then one of them started booting her motor,' he explained.

On hearing this, I've grabbed a bit of gear and made my way round to his house. Mick's in a right two 'n' eight as he explained in more detail exactly what happened and asked me how much I charged to have a word with these silly idiots. Mick was a very astute fella and had already done his home-work, quickly finding out that they were working out of some office block opposite the pub.

'I don't want you to do anything, John, just be with me in case, 'cos I ain't letting this go, no matter what happens – those men need their cards marking!'

What I never told Mick was that I had already had a nose around their gaff half an hour before, just to get a good look at the place. Mickey went in first, headed up the stairs and into this room. As we walked in the whole place just stopped and, all of a sudden, this one fella tries having it away on his toes, straight past me. Immediately, I've put my hand on him a bit heavy and said, "Ere, where do you think you're going? Get back up those stairs!' I followed Mick in and listened as he addressed the room, 'Right, you horrible lot, cast your minds back to last Monday when you came out of the pub and started harassing a woman as she was coming around the corner in a navy-blue Volkswagen motor. Now, don't start telling fucking porkies, or my man here will get upset!' he said, as I'm stand-ing behind him, slipping my gloves on. Anyway, one of these fellas' faces dropped as he's clocked me. He's starting to sweat like he's in the Sahara, and the colour has drained from his face. He immediately admits to being in the pub, but no more, so with that, Mickey says, 'Alright, who was the clever cunt who kicked the fucking window?'

At which point the fella that's doing all the talking starts to get a bit twitchy, he's absolutely shitting himself. Mind you, I ain't surprised given the kind of looks and scowls on my face that I'm giving the room.

'Ah, I don't know, what are you going to do to us?' the talkative fella asks.

'Look, I just want to know who it is. If my mate here was going to do anything to you, you'd already be on the other side of this window by now. Right, what's going to happen is this – you're going to give me your telephone number, and then I'm going to give you two days before I ring you. When I do, you're going to give me a number, it's that simple.'

Mr Talkative then asked Mickey if it was his wife in the car, to which Mickey replied, 'It's a friend of ours, and we don't take too kindly to this sort of bullying. Look, you've got two days to sort it, and if you come up with fuck-all, my man here will be paying you another visit.'

And with that, we left the office just in case they had secretly rung for the police. Mickey asked me how much he owed me for my services, but I told him I'd never charge him a penny, especially for this sort of thing, but he treats me to a bite to eat at Nando's just to say thank you.

Two days later, they called Mickey with a number, which he immediately rang up and gave them a warning. He also paid the bloke a visit round his house but could never catch him in – I'm guessing he'd heard about our little visit and stayed away.

I spent many a year and had some good times with my mate Kiran on the doors. Kiran was a proper doorman who had your back and would always be there for you at the drop of a hat. I first started working with him in Ealing, west London. We did some real rough venues so I would always make sure that I had my boxing pads with me, because with these sorts of clubs we knew that I'd be slipping them on regularly. In this one venue there used to be a tiny little door with a path outside that led to a fence by the road. The amount of people I smashed over that fence you couldn't count on ten hands.

One particular night in this bar, Kiran and I were having a walk around when a group of rugby players came in; these were all big lumps, but as is usually the case with rugby players not all of them are tasty with their fists. Anyway, they were starting to get rowdier by the minute, at which point Kiran and I went over to them and said, 'C'mon, lads, we don't mind you enjoy-ing yourselves, but calm it down a bit, don't take the piss.'

They didn't take the slightest bit of notice; they simply ignored us and carried on drinking, getting busy and throwing their weight around a bit. Kiran and I went over and pulled the biggest and loudest one out and gave him another warning, only this time, as is often the case, he took offence. He didn't take kindly to it because he said we made him look stupid. Now, like I said, these were some big strong fellas and there were at least eight of them in total. Immediately, one of them squared up into my face. He obviously wanted a fight, so I wasted no time at all and smashed him on the chin. He's gone reeling, but now it's gone tits up because the gang of them were going absolutely nuts. Unfortunately, there were only four of us working the whole place that night, and this little battle had turned into all-out war. Eventually, we managed to get them over to the front door and, with a bit more space, we're smashing them senseless – there was claret everywhere as we're putting them out. It was lucky that I had a good team around me who knew how to handle these situations. With our hands-on expertise, we managed to school them in the art of club brawling and sent them packing, all bust up like they'd played the last quarter against the Harlequins. Anyway, there were no threats of any comebacks from them, so that was the end of that.

Another rough house that I've talked about before was in Ealing. I was working down there one night when this fella came to the door, causing a bit of bother. Very discreetly, I've slipped on my gloves just to make sure that I was ready for him. I've warned him and warned him to calm down and insisted that he can't come in, no matter what. However, he still kept on and on with the mouth, getting braver and braver by the second. Now, most of the time it takes a lot to ruffle my feathers, but this man was starting to really get to me. How polite and amicable I seemed to be was obviously making him, in his boss-eyed state, mistake my kindness for weakness. Suddenly, Kiran's stepped up and said, 'Just go on your way, bruv, you ain't getting in, and the more leary you get, the worse you're making it, so jog the fuck on.'

With that, he's launched himself forward. I could clearly see that he was revving up for a strike, so I've immediately seen red and unloaded him. I'm smashing shots into him and, just like that, he's knocked out. I'm still in a rage so I'm on top of him, hitting him like some UFC fighter in a cage – there's blood all over the place and I'm still unloading on him. Kiran and the other doormen have seen that I've completely lost it and they've grabbed me to try and pull me away but, like I said, my head had completely gone, and I was screaming at them to get off me as well. I was in a madman zone – this man had wound me up so much that I smashed into him more because of his lack of respect. It didn't have to be like that – if he'd have just bloody listened.

Finally, I calmed myself down and walked back into the club, and I left the other doormen to deal with the aftermath of getting him moved. It was only when I calmed down that I realised how close I'd come to killing him, because my shirt and face were covered in blood like something out of a horror film. I waited for the Old Bill to arrive, but nothing came of it, and I heard no more.

It happens everywhere you go. Some nice people toe the line, but there's always the village idiot out. Another time, I was working on the door with Kiran at a well-known club in Mayfair. The place was full of famous people – actors, singers, sports personalities, we had them all coming in as it was a nice little place to go. Like I said, now and again you would get the occasional bout of trouble. One night, a bunch of blokes turned up on bikes. Anyway, we could see straight away that they were rowdy football fans, one of 'em wearing a West Ham top had a huge chip on his shoulder. I ain't generalising, but if there's a bunch of them, it's usually the one that's wearing his team's stripes that seems to want a row.

Right, so, he's started giving it the big one, he's telling us that he's coming in the club with his mates. We tried to explain that football tops were against our policy and that we don't allow the wearing of them in the club. But these men were having none of it. So, I said to Kiran laughing, as one of them pushes me in the chest with a bit of force, 'Shall I go first?' He's getting a bit leary, so I've gone outside and told him to piss off or he'll get hurt. And that's it, it's gone off! He's come at me and I've smashed him in the face, sending him flying to the floor. Kiran's smashed the other one, and they've stumbled off like the walking wounded with their mates holding them up.

In the early nineties, I became good friends with another doorman called Brian Chambers. Brian was working for this security company, driving the boss around to nightclubs and pubs, collecting money. He also worked in the company's office in north-west London, helping the business out with another mate of mine, Mikey Street. This company had about 250 doormen out on the doors all over London most evenings. When a job came up with the firm, they gave me a call.

Brian was only about fourteen stone, but the fella was sharp as a tack and streetwise. He was also a fantastic talker, and a straight talker at that. Brian and Mikey shared the head doorman slot at the time, and they had an amazing and stable team who stuck together like a pack of dogs; every last one of them had one another's backs, in and outside of work. In fact, Brian started training with me and the boys and I taught him a lot. Before he realised it, he was up to nearly sixteen stone.

Some of the places we were sent over the next few months were really rough. The owners would not even open until we had all turned up to do our shifts on the door. Granted, we were paid well but I actually believe we should have been paid even more for the amount of trouble we were always ironing out. However, like everywhere we worked, we always made sure that we had a top-drawer team around us just in case it got a bit too heavy. Us boys still boxed clever, and purely down to the extreme violence that was on offer, we made sure that we went to work together, and we all left together as well – if one man had a problem, it was a problem for the team.

We were over in Peckham one evening, working in a right grotty old place; we had been put in there because the other door team they hired couldn't handle it. The first night we were there, there was loads of trouble going on all over the place. We had five doormen downstairs dealing with a situation, then they threw some men out of the front doors and immediately chained them shut. Suddenly, there's commotion everywhere so I've gone down this flight of steps to see what's happening and noticed the doors were rocking back and forth so much that the chain was close to breaking.

'John, get up here quick!' Brian hollered.

I ran like a banshee back up the flight of stairs to see what Brian was hollering about. The next thing you know the glass on these big front doors has gone through – these silly idiots have only gone and blown the glass through with a shooter which, thankfully, has just managed to miss me by a few feet. I was lucky I didn't get shards of glass stuck in me. All of a sudden, everything went quiet and the lot of them scarpered, obviously scared in case the Old Bill turned up and pinched the lot of them.

Another job came into the office one day from an Irish man who owned a club over in Croydon, and he wanted to get a completely new door team at his place because, again, the ones that they had working there weren't doing their job very well. We seemed to be doing a lot of that – mopping up everyone else's mess. This bunch was apparently worse and were getting up to all sorts, robbing the place too, by all accounts, and the gaffa simply couldn't control them. He'd been watching these dodgy doormen and how they were running his business into the ground, and he just wanted them out.

First things first, before we could go in and clean the place up, we had to get rid of the current team. Now, these fellas ain't gonna go if we tickle 'em to death, so we had to go in there hands-on and physically take over the club, leaving the pathway clear to put our proper team in. The boys had covered all the exits, and I have gone in there first. Apparently, this head doorman was some sort of heavyweight boxer; a bare-knuckle fighter 'n' all the aces. Anyway, he's come at me and I've gone in with a left hook and ironed him out. A few others came steaming in, so I smashed into them too and, after the other boys had sorted the rest of them out, they had it away, broken and damaged, never to return.

The next few weeks seemed to be fight after fight. All the local travellers were playing merry hell in there and, to be quite honest, it got quite heavy a few times. These lumps would come in numbers. Every bloody week, a van would pull up and the boys and I would give it to them. We'd be smashing the lot inside, outside, it didn't matter, they all got it. In the end, we ironed the lot of them out. I think they had finally had enough and got tired of the spankings – it was relentless – every night knowing there would definitely be trouble. But, with people like Brian, Mickey, Phil and a few others around, we cleaned each and every one of these places up within a month – we never failed.

14
I COULD BE SO GOOD FOR YOU

Throughout the eighties and nineties, and on through to the present day, I worked as a bodyguard to some very famous people, not to mention a great many wealthy people too. My job wasn't quite as orthodox as those with paper credentials that you see in the world of close protection, no. The only licence that I held was the one that centred on my fist-fighting reputation – one that was talked about in whispers among the gangster elites from the murky depths of London's underworld for many years.

My credentials were earned on the blood-soaked streets, as I watched over the roughest and toughest pubs, clubs and gambling dens in the East End to the dazzling and glamour-soaked streets of the West End. Acting in the capacity of the bodyguard was a step up from what I was used to, and many of the people involved were of a more refined class, and the adornment of wealth enabled them to pay rather handsomely for my services.

From politicians to musicians and sporting greats to gamblers with high-stakes, I watched over them all. I even looked after one of the most famous men on the planet at the time, Mike Tyson. Look, I know what you're thinking, *Why the hell would Mike Tyson need a bodyguard*? Right? Well, I'll tell you.

This is London in the late eighties, with the onset of guns and knives, when every Tom, Dick, and Harry was out there trying to make a name for themselves. Although Mike could handle himself in a street brawl, it just isn't something his management would want for him and that right there is the sole reason they pay people such as me – a man who will have a tear up at the drop of a hat, and even in your back garden if that's what happens to be on offer.

I remember it like it was yesterday, this was shortly after he had won the heavyweight title in 1986 against Trevor Berbick. The first time he walked in the club and clocked me, he could not take his eyes off the size of my neck, at which point he started to laugh and commented on it to his mate.

Tyson had a nineteen-inch neck, and I imagine you can all remember what he looked like. Therefore, I'm sure you can see why he looked a little stunned at seeing me. I got on well with him for the next few nights while taking him round the clubs I was minding, and he would tell me about his fights on the cobbles when he was a young fella growing up. Mike was a lot different to the public's perception, fuelled by the media. Even at the tender age of twenty he was a listener, and he loved my stories, always showing great interest in regard to where I had been and what I had done. It was a memorable time for me, and I have recently been reconnected with Mike through our mutual friend, Joe Egan, so I'm hoping that we can meet up again soon in Vegas.

I had always fancied the sound of bodyguarding famous people from the stories Mick Kinane used to tell me. Mick had guarded boxers like Henry Cooper, along with a bevy of other celebrities that span across the globe. Back then, anyone and everyone knew the name Mick Kinane, and from the stories these fellas had told I knew there was a lot more money to be earned. A hell of a lot more than I was pulling in just standing on a club door, night in, night out, waiting for trouble.

So, a job came in, bodyguarding various snooker celebrities at tournaments all over London. I got to know the likes of Jimmy White and a whole collection of other big names; I even minded the late Alex Higgins, God rest his soul, and let me tell you this, that man certainly lived up to the nickname of The Hurricane. So, as I was working in Mayfair in the West End, they'd come down to the clubs and, while minding these people, I was looked after very well; many of them were very generous, splashing the cash about, not to mention the food was always top class, too, which was a massive bonus for me.

I started working for a big company that got me jobs all over London, including the Wembley Arena gig, where some prominent bands and singers were playing at the time. I got to get up close and personal with top people like Prince, and the rocking Canadian, Bryan Adams. One day I turned up to bodyguard Bryan, and as we were going up in the lift, I said to him, 'Hi, I'm John, I've just been asked to stay with you.'

He replied, 'It's OK, I don't want any bodyguards. I don't need them!'

To which I replied, ever so politely, 'Oh, I'll just stay out of the way, then. You won't even know I'm about.'

I honestly don't think he was being cocky. I think he was just of the opinion of all of us – who's going to want to hurt Bryan Adams? However, he was on my manor now and we had been hired by his manager to look after him, so that's exactly what we did. I stood on the side of the stage as he blasted through his hits and, once he came off, I watched on from just a few feet away, discretely following him around wherever he wanted to go. Bryan was a really nice guy, and despite his feelings towards being guarded, he always thanked me for watching him.

The shows continued to come in, from Soul II Soul to the soul sisters themselves, The Supremes, and everyone from Paul Young to Peter Andre. Here's a funny little story for you. I was working Wembley Stadium for The Rolling Stones, who were doing a big concert there. I arrived in the morning in my Discovery, but I was struggling to find a car parking space. Then I noticed this space – well, what I thought was a free space, but I'll get back to that one in just a moment. So, I've parked up and gone inside, and I've had my briefing as to my role that day and on through the next twelve hours or so. I was posted very close to Mick Jagger and the rest of the band; unfortunately, I didn't get the chance to talk to any of them. Anyway, the start of my brief was to meet them inside the building, but they were nowhere to be seen. All of a sudden, I heard them talking just around the corner from where I was stood, and I heard Mick telling one of the organisers that he'd been stuck in his limousine outside for over forty-five minutes because someone had parked their motor in a restricted area. Mr Jagger wasn't happy at all, believe me, especially given the fact that, due to security reasons, they couldn't leave their limo. The show went well, then it's all over, so I went back to my vehicle only to find that it wasn't bloody there. I'm thinking to myself, 'Right, c'mon, John, where the hell have you parked it?' And there I am, standing looking confused, rubbing my chin when this security guy comes up to me and says, 'You're not looking for your jeep, are you, mate?'

And I replied, 'Yes, it's disappeared, mate. I'm positive I parked it here.' The security fella goes on to explain that they had to get a tow truck in to move it because it was blocking the entrance where Mick Jagger's limo was supposed to come in. He then took me over to where they had put my car, and a true Shaggy out of *Scooby-Doo* style 'Yikes!' came into my mind. Wild horses couldn't have dragged me away any faster.

Another celebrity encounter I had was when I used to mind a place called Hanover Grand, which was a popular place that many celebrities would often frequent. One night we had Lennox Lewis, the heavyweight champion boxer, at the door, with Prince Naseem Hamed in tow. Lennox was a total gentleman, he shook my hand, and we had a chat. However, Prince Naseem just stood there poncing and prancing, doing his 'I'm the King of the Ring' bit. He kept on with this for a minute or two, and all the time I'm stood staring at him, thinking to myself, what do you look like, you silly idiot, at which point I said to him, 'Look, are you coming in, or you going to stand there poncing about all evening?'

Lennox immediately started laughing, and as he walked past me to enter the club, he gave me a 'this is uncomfortable' style of nod and a wink. Like I said, many stars would spend time at the club. Ricky Hatton was another that also used to come down to the West End for a night out. Ricky was a nice guy, he was at his biggest then, though; he must have been about five stone over his fighting weight at the time and, as well you all know, he loved a drop of the old booze.

But it wasn't always celebrities that needed minding. A job came up where I was asked to keep an eye on this man called Kassem Hammoud, whose father was a billionaire. It was a great little number – we would train in the mornings over at a gym in Cricklewood and, when we were done, I'd take him back and forth to meetings, making sure he was safe. I spent nearly a year with Kas, and we got on great. After a good few months, he asked would I look after his mother, who was on her way back from a trip abroad. Kas managed to persuade me, and it was on!

Mrs Hammoud took an immediate liking to me and wanted me to be her permanent driver. I think I must have done it for about four weeks until she got a little too demanding; it got to the stage where I couldn't even have my food breaks. I'd take her shopping and drop her off, then I'd get a little bit of a break and I'd try and eat my rice and chicken a bit lively before she came back. However, I wasn't quick enough because, in no time at all, she was on her way back, so I'd have to sling all the food straight in the boot of the motor. What with me being a bit OCD, it was doing my nut in.

'Kas, this is getting way too much for me. When can I come back with you?' I asked him one day.

'But John, you can't, my mum likes you. She thinks you're the best driver she's had. Sorry, mate.'

But in the end, I couldn't take it no more and ended up finishing up with her. I thought to myself, I know she likes me, but she'll have to like me from a distance.

Last, but certainly not least, I want to give a shout-out to another good mate of ours, the late Billy Isaac. Bill was an ex-professional boxer who feared no man. The last place I ever worked in, in London, was Billy's lap-dancing club in Mayfair, known as No: 4. Bill was in awe of Lenny; he even had his car number plate (BI GUV) done in dedication. Billy used to praise Lenny, and he would say to me, 'You grew up with Lenny, John. I'm not having these people saying a bad word about him. All these youngsters saying they're The Guv'nor, for fuck's sake, I'll smash the fucking lot of them!'

I was playing about one day, sparring with Billy, and as I was unloading a few shots, Bill said, 'Fucking hell, John, I can see Lenny in you, the way you use your hands.' I immediately thanked him; it was a nice compliment, particularly as Len was no longer with us.

This brings me to a nice little evening we had when Bill asked me and a few others, Kev Sumer included, to go to an unlicenced boxing event staged by Joey Pyle junior. Apparently, this fella, Gary Sayer, was fighting for The Guv'nor title. So, Billy said to us, 'I'm going to go down there to watch this fight, and then I'm going to fight him because no way should he be having Lenny's fucking title. I'm going to knock him spark out.'

Bill also said that he was going to win the belt and hold it until someone worthy came along who actually deserved its ownership. So, anyway, Bill says to the pair of us, 'Right, you two, I want you on your best behaviour, no fucking fighting.'

Kev and I were looking at each other laughing, saying, ''Ere, Bill, when do we ever start a row? Granted we always finish 'em, but we only fight when we have to!'

So, we've all gone down there about twenty-handed, and as we walked into the foyer, the doorman goes off to get Joey, and Joey says to Bill, 'I can let you in for free, Bill, but I can't let all the rest of them in too.'

Bill replied, 'You trying to fucking mug me off in front of my pals, Joey? Now get out of my fucking way!'

Bill barged him out of the way with us lot following up, but he did tell us all to behave ourselves.

Now, having been in the gaff for at least a minute, this Sayer spots Bill and comes marching over like a bull, trying to look intimidating, and says to him, 'Alright, Isaacs, are me and you going to have it soon, then?'

Next thing you know, Billy has smashed him, and the place has gone right up. Our lot have all gone steaming in, tables are flying everywhere, and it's absolute chaos with the doormen and the rest of them. By this time, Bill made his way outside and he's screaming at the poor doorman, 'Get that fat cunt out here, we'll have it on the cobbles.'

Anyway, we've gone outside to front it with Billy and, fortunately for this Sayer fella, when we got out there, we managed to calm Bill down a bit. Not long after, he went back inside, got himself into the ring, and did a heartfelt speech about Lenny and The Guv'nor title. The title that he wanted back for Len, reiterating to the crowd that he would fight the winner of the next match to bring the belt home. Kev stayed behind to watch his cousin box, but the rest of us went up the pub without even watching the Sayer fight. From what we were told by Kev later we hadn't missed a great deal. Apparently, Kev shouted all sorts of abuse at this Sayer bloke, saying the bloke he was fighting against was half his size and he couldn't even put him away. Kev said a ten-year-old could've hit harder – he was a big, useless lump. It's a shame the fight never came off because it meant so much to Bill for him to reclaim Len's title.

It wasn't long after this event that Billy had a terrible accident at his home in Durrus, west of Cork. He had locked himself out and had fallen badly when trying to climb in through a window, and he died aged just forty-five.

Like I've stated all the way through my story, our lads were the real deal and a formidable bunch if you ever crossed us. We also always had a laugh and a joke, even with the punters, unless anyone mistook our kindness for weakness and turned a joke into a row, at which point all bets were off, and they'd quickly see the other side of any one of us.

15
NOT SO GRIM UP NORTH

It was around 2013 that I decided I needed a bit of a change. I'd had enough of the hundred-mile-an-hour London life. The Smoke, as it is referred to far and wide, had become unrecognisable to me, and the safe haven I had once called home had spiralled into a disjointed, lost city. I seriously needed to switch things up. The clubland was full to the brim with wannabe gangster types looking for a row at any given moment, to make a name for themselves, or simply to further their valueless reputation.

I searched and searched for quite some time before settling on the idea that Lincolnshire seemed like a scenic and tranquil place to lay my hat. In addition to that, I had family and friends dotted around which, of course, was an absolute bonus. Another big plus point was the cost of living; this was something that could only be seen as a massive pull to me and my move away from Britain's capital.

With a heavy heart, and a little less heavy bank balance, I packed up my belongings and made the journey; a journey that, years ago, I would have completely denied myself. I found a nice little homely place to start me off, which was great, and even more importantly, I found a gym so that, in no time at all, I started to make a select set of new friends.

Shortly after arriving in Lincolnshire, I was in the gym and got chatting to this fella who was keen to know where I was originally from. At that time, I didn't have a clue who the hell I was talking to, I simply told people that back in London I was known as John the Neck; at which point this particular individual promptly replied, 'Fuck me, so you're "The Neck", you're the man who was friends with Lenny McLean, aren't you?'

It was apparent from his reply that he had heard stories about me from my new mates in the area.

Life up here has been a hell of a lot calmer; I haven't even had to unload anybody for a good few years. As luck would have it, life has been relatively trouble-free. Well, apart from the odd silly idiot that seems to follow me around. So, here I am today. It's 2018 and I'm still breathing, still ducking and diving, trying to make my way in the world. I've gone from owning two beautiful houses in the city suburbs, with jeeps and motorbikes in my possession and a good amount of cash on the hip, to this – the way life is today. I'm still working hard to scratch a living, albeit with slightly less cash and assets. At one time I had a lovely house until my son's mother and I split in 1999. I'm always in touch with Dana, the 'Hostess with the Mostess', and my son, James, and his beautiful baby girl, my granddaughter, Alaska. This little bunch, a prospector's gold pan of dreams, have been, and will always be, my special little family unit, and nothing on God's earth will ever change that.

I did meet another woman a few years later, and we bought a house together in 2006. We eventually went our separate ways in 2011. I was left with absolutely nothing.

I'm still in touch with a lot of my old work colleagues, and still speak to a great deal of them, but many others, like myself, have moved away. Those who I do stay in close contact with would be there for me at the drop of a hat, just as I would for them.

I still spend a lot of time down the gym; I'm committed to keeping in shape. Sometimes I'm happy with it and sometimes it gets me down. If, for instance, I catch some kind of illness, maybe a cold or whatever, it puts my gym routine back a bit, sometimes by a few days or more, and this isn't good for my programme, diet, or my mental state. My mental wellbeing is affected by this because my mind is geared towards a rigid set of goals, and my fitness plays a huge part in that. For people who don't train, they just wouldn't understand this. You have to be involved in building the body to have an understanding of it. Which brings me to the lack of knowledge and education around the use and abuse of steroids.

You cannot, and will not, sit on your sofa or relax by a pool, take a fistful of steroids and turn yourself into Bertil Fox, Arnie or the Hulk, Lou Ferrigno, because in order to build muscle, you must be dedicated to working your mind, body, and soul to achieve your goals.

The other side to life down the gym is the social aspect and, for me, I meet and have become friends with some of the best people you could ever wish to meet; strong-willed, determined and, above all, dedicated, and this for me is a recipe for a well-rounded person. The gym is the place where I started, and it will be the place I finish and, let's face it, there aren't many places where you can keep fit, socialise and get a bit of work, so I'm pleased to be a part of it.

I've been let down on many occasions but, as the great crooner Frank Sinatra himself said, 'That's life,' and, God willing, I will be back on top very soon.

Joking apart, all of this has a bittersweet feel to it for me. The bitter bit is not having Lenny, Andy Jones, Paul O'Loughlin, and some of my other pals here to share it with. But, if I'm honest, it's my parents, Mum and Dad, that really saddens me; they never really knew the extent of what I managed to achieve.

If my dad was still around, it would have been nice to be a fly on the wall 'cos I can picture him now, with my book in his hand, a faint smile flickering across his face as he read about my time spent minding a certain celebrity. I'd like to think that Dad was proud of me in his own little way but, like the majority of the stiff-upper-lip brigade from his generation, he simply had a hard time showing it.

I sit here today, alone and on tenterhooks, waiting for a phone call about a job that would see me back in the concrete jungle, my old home in London, and on to the next instalment of my life. This life is part of my makeup, where I am comfortable, and, lastly, a place where everybody knows the name, John the Neck.

Photo credit: Lee Wortley